# A WALK TO FREEDOM

**The Reverend Fred Shuttlesworth and the
Alabama Christian Movement for Human Rights, 1956-1964**

Marjorie L. White

*Published by*
Birmingham Historical Society

Birmingham Historical Society
White, Marjorie L.
Includes index.
1. Alabama Christian Movement for Human Rights. 2. Rev. Fred Lee Shuttlesworth 3. Baptists—
United States—Clergy 4. African-Americans—Civil Rights
ISBN (softback) 0-943994-24-1
Library of Congress 98-74154

ORIGINAL LIMITED EDITION

Cover Illustration:
"5/4/1963-Birmingham, AL – During a mass rally of more than 3,000 Negroes protesting segregation, these three demonstrators hold hands for strength against the water." Original UPI caption; UPI/Corbis Bettmann Archive U1378208-29. Reprinted with permission.

# Table of Contents

# Introduction

## Marjorie L. White

I moved to Birmingham 30 years ago, shortly after the events described in this book occurred. Not long after coming to Birmingham, I became interested in the history of the Birmingham area, particularly the history of its industrial and commercial development and its architecture and urban planning. Frequently, I heard, "I did not realize Birmingham had a history. It is too young to have a history." "History" to these commentators meant white columned antebellum houses of which Birmingham has but one remaining example. I have found that Birmingham has a rich and important history in many areas, and I have written about some of them. However, while important things happened in Birmingham in its first 100 years, by far the most significant aspect of its history is the civil rights conflict that occurred in the period 1956 to 1964.

Even with the passage of many years, the story of racial conflict in Birmingham still evokes pain and reticence. To some, it is a story that should not be further told, a tale too painful and too damaging to community self-esteem to be repeated. For others, the story has to be told repeatedly in order to exorcize the painful effects of the events of the early sixties. This book explores a different theme. It celebrates the civil rights conflict in Birmingham and rejoices in the triumph that occurred in the midst of tragedy.

"But for Birmingham, we wouldn't be here." So stated President John F. Kennedy during the summer of 1963. "Here" was a meeting at the White House to plan what became the Civil Rights Act of 1964. This Act, together with the Voting Rights Act of 1965, confirmed the change in the moral, social and political climate of America. The 1964 Act mandating equality in public accommodations and employment was inspired by the Birmingham demonstrations of April and May 1963. Its passage was made inevitable by the murder of Medgar Evers and others, by the assassination of President Kennedy and by the sacrifice of four young lives in the September 1963 bombing of Birmingham's Sixteenth Street Baptist Church. That bombing was motivated by the role of that church as the starting point of many 1963 demonstrations that provoked attacks on the demonstrators with fire hoses and police dogs.

The 1963 demonstrations were primarily the work of the Alabama Christian Movement for Human Rights (ACMHR) and the Rev. Fred L. Shuttlesworth, its leader who invited the Rev. Martin Luther King, Jr., and the Southern Christian Leadership Conference to participate in the Birmingham demonstrations. The attacks with fire hoses and police dogs were anticipated: the demonstrators were trained to respond nonviolently. Even an occurrence as horrendous as the Sixteenth Street Baptist Church bombing was understood as a possible consequence of ACMHR's struggle for freedom and equality. Shuttlesworth himself was the target of two bomb attacks and countless other threats and physical abuse. ACMHR knew the price that had be paid for freedom:

We know that the struggle will be hard and costly; some of us indeed may die; but let our trials and death — if come they must — be one more sacred installment on this American heritage for freedom; and let History and they that come behind us, rejoice that we arose in strength, armed only with the weapon of Love, and stood where men stood, and removed from American society this cancerous infection of Segregation and 2nd class citizenship (From "The New Negro Church," speech by Rev. Fred Shuttlesworth, Prayer Pilgrimage, Washington, D.C., May 17, 1957).

For seven years prior to the events in the spring of 1963, despite numerous church bombings and constant threats and intimidation from the KKK and police, Shuttlesworth and the ACMHR created the strongest Southern civil rights organization and challenged every local segregation law. ACMHR was led by Shuttlesworth's Bethel Baptist Church and 59 other black churches, whose membership of preachers, deacons, Sunday school teachers, secretaries and blue collar workers supported the organization with pennies or, at most, a dollar or two a week.

Shuttlesworth was viewed as an extremist, not just by Birmingham's white power structure, but by middle- and upper-class blacks as well and, at times, by the President of the United States and Martin Luther King, Jr., himself. Shuttlesworth's confrontational stance was foreshadowed by the theologian Reinhold Niebuhr in his 1932 book, *Moral Man and Immoral Society:*

A favorite counsel of the social scientists is that of accommodation. If two parties are in a conflict, let them, by conferring together, moderate their demands and arrive at a *modus vivendi.* . . . Undoubtedly there are innumerable conflicts which must be resolved in this fashion. But will a disinherited group, such as the Negroes for instance, ever win full justice in society in this fashion? (p. xvii)

Since reason is always, to some degree, the servant of interest in a social situation, social injustice cannot be resolved by moral and rational persuasion alone, as the educator and social scientist usually believes. Conflict is inevitable, and in this conflict power must be challenged by power. (p. xv)

It was Shuttlesworth's genius that he knew that his antagonist, Commissioner of Public Safety Theopholis Eugene "Bull" Connor, and Connor's backers, could be provoked to reveal qualities of cruelty and inhumanity that would undermine his cause. It was ACMHR's strength as an organization that emboldened the demonstrators, including school children, to face the fire hoses and police dogs without violence in return, to arise "in strength, armed only with the weapon of Love. . . . "

The civil rights conflict in Birmingham was not, as some believe, a mistake. It was the result of disciplined, principled, and strategically brilliant action by a network of inspired working-class, churchgoing people led by their pastors. Neither is the conflict a cause for shame.  Rather, it is to be celebrated as a magnificent achievement of the human spirit. Few times in our history has a group of ordinary men and women risked life and limb so unremittingly for the purpose of achieving liberty and equality.

Birmingham can be proud that its citizens won their fight for freedom on its streets.

• • • • •

Today's Birmingham is vastly different than that of the late 1950s and early 1960s. A thriving metropolis of almost one million people, Birmingham has evolved economically and socially. In addition to remaining an important industrial location, Birmingham has emerged as an international center for medical research, treatment and technology; engineering and construction, and as a regional financial center. The initial success of the Mercedes-Benz International manufacturing facility at nearby Vance holds out the promise that Birmingham may well become a center of automobile manufacturing as well.

Birmingham elected its first African American mayor, Richard Arrington, Jr., in 1979, before New York, Chicago, Baltimore or Philadelphia. Reform of the police force was the issue that brought Arrington to the position he retains to this day.

When visiting Birmingham, one can see the epicenter of America's Civil Rights Movement which includes the Bethel Baptist Church, the Fourth Avenue Business District, the Birmingham Civil Rights Institute and Sixteenth Street Baptist Church, as well as other places mentioned in this book. The map inserted in this volume is a guide to these places.

The Birmingham Civil Rights Institute, a $12 million dollar facility on Kelly Ingram Park, opened in 1992. The Institute's 28,000 square feet of exhibitions document the struggle of African-American citizens to become full participants in the city's government and business community. Seminars and programs feature nationally known scholars, performers and civil rights leaders. A research center collects records and documents. Each Monday morning, Operation New Birmingham's Community Affairs Committee (CAC), the biracial group formed just following the May 10, 1963 truce that ended the Birmingham demonstrations, meets to review racial issues in the community.

Since 1993, Birmingham Historical Society, working at times with the Historic American Engineering Record and the Historic American Building Survey (Washington, D. C. based documentation branches of the National Park Service), has conducted field work and archival research resulting in histories, photographs and measured drawings of significant Birmingham Civil Rights Churches. The full Park Service documentation was completed for Bethel Baptist Church and Sixteenth Street Baptist Church. The Society has conducted additional field surveys and archival research on the Movement-era churches and is currently seeking National Historic Landmark status for the Bethel and Sixteenth Street Baptist churches. The Society anticipates nominating all Movement-era churches to the National Register of Historic Places. Former ACMHR secretary Lola Hendricks served as mentor for the identification of the 60 Movement Meeting Churches. Many other individuals, most especially Rev. Shuttlesworth, have assisted with preparation of this book which summarizes the Birmingham Movement.

This volume reflects the Movement perspective. The story is told as a pictorial chronology, weaving together photographic images, Rev. Shuttlesworth's speeches and Annual Reports to the ACMHR as well as the local and national press accounts. The action takes place in the context of the Christian church, actually a network of 60 churches spread across the industrial city. This is a remarkable story of people of stalwart faith who believed that God would help them in their all-out, non-violent confrontation to banish segregation. They walked together, endured and suffered, until Freedom was won for all through the passage of the Civil Rights Act of 1964.

# Preface

## Rev. Fred Lee Shuttlesworth

This well researched documentation of the Alabama Christian Movement For Human Rights is a marvelous work by the Birmingham Historical Society and its Director, Marjorie White, and her excellent staff assisted immeasurably by Lola Hendricks, the Movement Clerical Secretary, who was present at its beginning and knew intimately all aspects of the Civil Rights "Foot Soldiers" and of the Birmingham Civil Rights Institute. It is an educational treatise about a group of ordinary people, oppressed Negroes, who rose up, fired by the Spirit of Truth, Righteousness and Justice; who suffered and persevered in challenging, changing, and finally overcoming Legal Segregation in Birmingham and the South. How wonderful this detailed History — sought and put together after 40 years — of those Negroes, never full citizens, who were not interested in keeping records of their deeds, nor recording history, or making names for themselves; but, who under Divine Compulsion, just wanted – and fought for – real freedom for themselves and their countrymen. In fact, any records kept by any organization fighting against Segregation in those days were subject to official seizure, unlimited harassment, and persecution by the System of its leaders, followers, and participants—as is shown by the injunction outlawing the NAACP, the event which caused ACMHR to come into being. This volume is not only good for inspirational and educational Value; it also fills a necessary void in the Documentation of some Writers who wrote their interpretations of the Movement's climactic days of Demonstrations. Had there been no beginning in simple faith and courage, there would have been no crescendo of climactic events to record!

Legal Segregation and Discrimination replaced the old Southern Colonial system of slavery in the South during which Blacks had absolutely no rights at all — even to exist. Segregation acknowledged their existence only; but absolutely no right to equal citizenship! And the everlasting Barriers against exact and equal rights for Negroes were the Ku Klux Klan, the Citizens Councils, Sovereignty Commissions, all Southern elected Officials of the States and National government, and the myriad legal machinery of the Law and the Courts! What an awesome array of condescending, never ending power! They thought neither God nor any earthly power could change it! To them, "God did it Himself, making different races and colors!"

No person of sound mind can truthfully impute God's Righteousness and Grace to the sinful and wicked reign of Segregation. But they preached and practiced it for generations! That Segregation prohibited initiative and creative manhood among Negroes is aptly shown by a 74-year-old man, who was arrested and in the cell with me and others after the second Bus Rides of 1958. He was thoroughly excited and happy, and said to me, "Reverend, I feel better today than at anytime in my life! I am 74-years-old today, and being arrested with you for freedom, I, just this day, found a reason for living!"

Many were the incidents that demonstrated the deep and burning desire for freedom, the loyalty, commitment, and lack of fear, among the people of the Movement, although danger and death forever stalked our lives. One will suffice here. Most times I was driven by guards and Movement people to rallies and other places. But one night, in the darkest and most menacing days of 1958-60, I drove my own car and parked it beside Rev. Abraham Woods' Church on the Southside, with the guards being outside for every Movement meeting. Upon dismissal that night, I got into my car with the door open and put the key in the switch to start it. Suddenly, abruptly, and with rough force, I was grabbed by my neck and shoulders and jerked from the car! Wondering if the Klan had suddenly overcome the guards, I looked up into the face of Will "John L. Lewis" Hall. He shoved me quickly into another guard's arms, immediately got into my car, turned the key in the switch and started the car. "John," I said to him, "What is the difference in my starting the car and your starting it?" Without hesitation he said, "you got to stay alive and lead us to our freedom! If I get killed, that's all right; I'm a nobody; but if you get killed now, who will lead us to freedom? No, God, we can't let nothing happen to you!"

In my heart that night I felt and fully knew the desire and need of people to be free! And as Paul wrote in 1 Timothy 1:12, "I thank God for putting me into this (leadership) Ministry, and enabling (sustaining) me." I praise God for that glorious little Bethel Baptist Church, bombed twice by the Klan under my administration — yet without a murmuring or complaining word — that carried on faithfully as I was away one third of the Sundays in 1957 and 1958 speaking for freedom, raising funds for bomb damage, rebuilding the Parsonage, and for the Movement; and which Church I rate in History with Old North Church in Boston, whose lights flashed and whose bell sounded the freedom alarm for the 1776 Ride of Paul Revere. Yes, thank God for Bethel and for Birmingham Negroes who rose up and walked with destiny into a new day! Thank God for the few Preachers and Churches who started the Movement and Others who joined! I thank the God of this Universe, Who purposed and planned it so, that the Kennedys were in the White House seat of power while the followers of Martin Luther King, Jr., Myself, and Other Leaders, were in the Streets, protesting, suffering, non violently, overfilling the jails, bitten by Bull Connor's dogs and washed by his powerful hoses, until the Powers of Government became concerned about and engaged with the people and their efforts for freedom and justice!!!

America traditionally honors its soldiers who offer their lives on fields of battle! Who deserve to be honored more than the unheralded Black Men and Women—and especially the courageous young Black School Children, without whom the battle would not have been won—on the segregated battlefield of Birmingham? Charity begins at Home; so should honor, and respectful acceptance, and freedom, and justice! Let the textbooks of this yet unfulfilled American day, and tomorrow, include the Truth of The Birmingham Movement, and its significance to our Country. Let the American Mindset move us all into the 21st century, committed to ending Racism, ending Violence, embracing EACH OTHER IN LOVE AND BROTHERHOOD. For, Blessed Is The Nation Whose God Is The Lord!

# The Historical Significance of Birmingham

## Rev. Wyatt Tee Walker

Birmingham, Alabama's, claim to fame prior to Martin Luther King's advent on the American scene was two-tiered. It was heralded as the South's largest industrial center and held the dubious distinction of being the South's *biggest and baddest* city in race relations. People of African ancestry were held in a vise-like grip of social and economic deprivation. The power structure of the city, prior to 1963, was a willing partner in maintaining the *status quo* of segregation forever. Even as industrial giants of the North and of the South began to invest their considerable resources in the development of Birmingham in the early 20th century, the mind-set was anti-union, anti-Catholic and of course, anti-Black.

As in other segregated communities across the South, the humanity of people of African ancestry survived (barely) through its internally developed infrastructure of religious life and business enterprises restricted to Black life principally. People of color in Birmingham, Alabama, entertained little thought of where the mainstream was located and no hope to be a part of it.

Then, without prior warning of any sort, the Reverend Fred Lee Shuttlesworth became the pastor of the Bethel Baptist Church. Bethel, under Shuttlesworth's courageous leadership (detailed in this volume), became the germ-center of a human rights struggle that would claim international attention and forever change the landscape of both social and political demographics of the entire South. I am aware that is a large claim but it is verified by any cursory or intense view of America's South land *before Birmingham* or *post Birmingham*. The specific reference is to the campaign of 1963 orchestrated jointly by the Alabama Christian Movement for Human Rights and the Southern Christian Leadership Conference. All pundits, informed and uniformed, are in agreement that the Birmingham movement is the chief watershed of the nonviolent movement in the United States. It marked the maturation of SCLC as a national force in the civil right arena of the land that had been dominated by the older and stodgier NAACP. It catapulted Shuttlesworth into an acceptability and credibility that had eluded him for too long despite his tenacity and courage.

Shuttlesworth's ACMHR was born in the wake of Alabama racists outlawing the NAACP. It became *a voice crying in the wilderness* and Shuttlesworth was its major prophet. SCLC, formed in 1957 in the wake of the highly successful Montgomery Bus Protest, had sputtered organizationally until 1960. Its supportive role in CORE's Freedom Ride and the Albany campaigns gave promise of what it might become. Birmingham's intransigence to ACMHR's moderate demands provided the *Zeitgeist* for a history-making movement. King and Shuttlesworth frequently disagreed on strategy on the southern scene, but Birmingham brought them together in a marvelous amalgam of mind and spirit. Sometimes, the road was bumpy, but the religious mooring of the Movement made *the rough places plain*.

Some chroniclers of the Birmingham era infer that the King/Shuttlesworth alliance was an uneasy one; not so! Its value was that the alliance was *dynamic*. These two activist giants nourished each other with their respective strengths and weaknesses. Birmingham could never have become what it was without Martin Luther King, Jr,. and Fred Lee Shuttlesworth. The two organizations complemented each other; the solid-rock character of the ACMHR on the local scene provided the endurance for a such a campaign and SCLC's professional staff, some with considerable skills and experience, provided the know-how to keep the nation's and the world's attention fixed on Birmingham. Together they produced a *fire that the water could not put out!*

The central historical significance of the Birmingham movement was alluded to earlier: . . . *became the germ-center of a human right struggle that would claim international attention and forever change the landscape of both social and political demographics of the entire South.* That is to say that Birmingham does not stand alone; Birmingham made Selma *possible!* The two movements, one social, altered with the *Public Accommodations bill* the social demographics of the South. Segregation by custom and legal fiat was completely dismantled. The Selma March swung the nation's attention to the fundamental right of a democracy, the unfettered *right to vote!* The *Voting Rights bill* changed the political demographics of the South forever. It freed Whites politically as much as it did Blacks. These two occurrences joined at the hip as Siamese twins changed forever the social and political landscape of the Deep South where intermarriage was once illegal and no person of African ancestry had ever voted in Sunflower County, Mississippi. Birmingham killed segregation and Selma committed the body. The compelling reality is that there could have been no Selma had there not been a Birmingham. It was the sheer power of Birmingham that convinced John F. Kennedy to make a 180 degree turn on the issue of civil rights. In January, the President of the United States declared his earnest view that no additional civil rights legislation was needed. In June of the same year on network television and radio, he made an impassioned plea for the nation to make this *moral decision.* The result was the introduction of what became the 1964 *Public Accommodations bill.* The passage of that bill established the King movement as an authentic American revolution and SCLC as a legitimate player in the pantheon of civil rights giants. Thus, SCLC's leadership in the Selma campaign was unquestioned. Nonviolence's full credibility was firmly established in the Birmingham campaign and the shadow of King's leadership was immeasurably lengthened with the awarding of the Nobel Prize for Peace in December 1964. The Movement overnight had become internationalized and Birmingham had played a critical role in this new dimension of race relations politics in America.

*Dr. Wyatt Tee Walker, Senior Minister, Canaan Baptist Church of Christ, New York, NY served as Chief of Staff to Dr. Martin Luther King, Jr. and Architect for Project C, April-May, 1963.*

# Shelter in a Storm—
# The African American Church in Birmingham

## Rev. Wilson Fallin, Jr.

From the beginning of black migration into Birmingham in the late 1800s, the church was the foundation institution in the African American community. It provided many functions. Most of all, it was a spiritual institution which met the religious needs of blacks in the city. Given only the dirtiest and most unskilled jobs, relegated to the worst housing areas and viewed by whites as inferior, African Americans found little in the community to give them worth, dignity and self-esteem. The church was the one place blacks could feel good about themselves. They were deacons, trustees, ushers, choir members and heads of organizations. In the church, they were somebody and respected. As a spiritual institution, the church was the place where African Americans could go and escape the hostility of the white world in Birmingham. There they could express their deepest thoughts and highest hopes. Key to black self-esteem, hope, and self-respect was the preaching of their pastors. Through sermons such as "Moses at the Red Sea," "Dry Bones in the Valley" and "The Eagle Stirreth Her Nest," blacks could identify their plight with the Old Testament Israelites and know that God was working on their behalf.

As African Americans moved into Birmingham (founded in 1871 to be the industrial center of the South), the church served not only their moral and spiritual needs but also was in the forefront of establishing institutions to meet their physical and secular needs in a segregated city. As the central institution in black communities, churches supported and enhanced the other institutions established by African Americans in the city. Because of pastors' unique role in the churches, they became the key leaders in the wider community. Using their churches as a base, they established institutions to fill the economic, educational and welfare needs of African Americans in the city. For example, in 1890, Rev. William R. Pettiford, pastor of the Sixteenth Street Baptist Church, founded the first black bank in the city which provided the funds for black home ownership and the many businesses established in the city between 1890 and 1915. Although Rev. Pettiford and other pastors did not make a frontal attack on segregation, they criticized and protested against what they saw as the abuses of the Jim Crow system in Birmingham.

By 1956, the African American church and its pastors were in the best position to project a mass-based movement against the vicious segregation which existed in Birmingham. Churches touched every segment of the African American community, the masses and the middle-class alike. There was a common church culture. By 1956, there were at least 400 African American churches in Birmingham and Jefferson County, located in every African American community. People in the black community generally respected ministers, and ministers had a history of leadership in the community. These factors made possible mobilization of large numbers of persons.

In 1956, the African American church in Birmingham initiated a movement to free blacks from the oppression and rigid segregation that they faced in the city. Led by a courageous pastor, Rev. Fred Shuttlesworth, who set the tone and direction of the movement, and buttressed by a strong faith in God, the Alabama Christian Movement for Human Rights struggled to eliminate segregation in Birmingham. In 1963, the movement brought the Rev. Martin Luther King, Jr., to the city and organized massive demonstrations that captured the attention of the nation and led to the passage of the Civil Rights Act of 1964.

*Rev. Wilson Fallin, Jr. is President of the Birmingham Baptist Bible College, a member of the history faculty at the University of Montevallo and author of* Shelter in the Storm–The African American Church in Birmingham, Alabama, 1815-1963, *a 1995 Ph.D.dissertation, soon to appear in paperback.*

# A WALK TO FREEDOM

# "A Walk With Destiny to Freedom and First Class Citizenship" Begins

*Rev. Fred Lee Shuttlesworth, Danny Lyon, Magnum Photos, Inc.*

**The Alabama Christian Movement for Human Rights** organizes to "press forward for Freedom and Democracy and the removal from our society of any forms of Second Class Citizenship." On May 26, 1956, the state of Alabama had temporarily outlawed the National Association for the Advancement of Colored People. The NAACP had championed rights and voting privileges since its founding in 1909. ACMHR organized to fill this void.

## A Tough Leader for a Tough Town

The Civil Rights Movement of the 1950s and 1960s was a ministerial-led movement. One of the "best and brightest" of its youthful leaders, Rev. Fred Lee Shuttlesworth was of humble and working class origin. His leadership style was aggressive and confrontational. His preaching style was emotional.

Rev. Shuttlesworth told his story with fiery words and gestures "until folks were jumping across the aisles." In the photograph above, outspread arms proclaim that, "When you squeeze in from both sides, it's hell! On the one side are the Klan and the police and on the other side, those Negroes — middle class preachers, middle ground friends and those that go about their business — who should be with you and who are not."

*But I organized to fight segregation. (I put this in their hearts and in their minds that night.) Now when you organize to fight segregation, that means you can never be still. We're gonna wipe it out, or it's gonna wipe us out. Somebody may have to die.* – Rev. Fred Lee Shuttlesworth, *Ebony,* 1971.

# Negroes roar approval at rights meeting

Reprinted from *The Birmingham News,* June 6, 1956, Page 1 & 11

An organization pledged to sweeping away "any forms of second class citizenship" was formed here last night amid roars of an estimated 1,000 Negroes approving a "march to complete freedom."

The "Alabama Christian Movement for Human Rights" was established at a mass meeting of Negroes at Sardis Baptist Church.

Negro ministers told the overflow crowd the new organization may provide leadership for Negroes over Alabama and possibly the entire South. Speakers declared it has no connection with the National Association for the Advancement of Colored People.

The meeting was announced after Circuit Judge Walter B. Jones granted an injunction at Montgomery Friday restraining the NAACP from operating in Alabama, but a spokesman said it had been set before that date.

The Rev. F. L. Shuttlesworth, one of the ministers who called the meeting, was named president by acclamation.

The Rev. R. L. Alford, pastor of the Sardis Baptist Church, 1240 Fourth St. N., estimated 1,000 to 1,100 Negroes attended the meeting. The church has a seating capacity of about 850, he said, and there were a number of persons standing.

Rev. Shuttlesworth, the principal speaker, declared: "The Citizens Councils won't like this. But then, I don't like a lot of things they do."

---

*I always have felt that the preacher is God's first man. . . .The prophets of old give us vivid examples of how the Church stands up and when they stand up the walls must fall. . . . I think that's what Christ meant by the 'gates of Hell shall not prevail.' It didn't mean, in my opinion, a man or gambler or wicked institution triumphant over the Church, but it meant the Church triumphant over them, because the people would be inspired to go out and crusade against it.*
– Rev. Shuttlesworth to Lewis Jones, 1961.

The young Negro preacher frequently raised his voice to a shout during his speech and mopped his face with a handkerchief. A thermometer near the pulpit read 88 degrees.

At the close of his address, Rev. Shuttlesworth introduced the Rev. N. H. Smith, Jr., who read a report of a committee which met Monday.

The committee report, containing a resolution naming the organization and setting forth its aims was adopted with a roar of approval.

One dissenting vote was cast, that of a man who identified himself as G. W. McMurray. He obtained the floor later and declared: "We should think sanely of what we are doing. Birmingham is too over-organized now." He cited another organization of Negro ministers formed several months ago.

Rev. Shuttlesworth replied, "If it takes one organization five months to get a constitution, what are we going to do!"

The speaker was interrupted a number of times by cheers and applause. The good-natured audience also encouraged him with frequent cries of "Yes, yes," "Go ahead, Reverend," and "That's right."

In his impassioned plea for organized Negro leadership, the speaker declared, "Our citizens are reactive under the dismal yoke of segregation." Then, he shouted, "Aren't you," and the crowd, roared "Yes."

"These are the days when men would like to kill hope, when men in Mississippi can be declared 'not guilty' (of murder), when men can be shot down on the steps of the courthouse. These are dark days.

"But hope is not dead. Hope is alive here tonight," he said.

He shouted, "We seek nothing which we would not deny others."

He asked, "Would you be willing tonight for a white man to sit down beside you?"

The audience again roared assent.

"Then you believe in integration," Rev. Shuttlesworth declared.

The lengthy resolution adopted near the close of the meeting was prepared by a committee of 11 ministers and laymen.

"HANDS UP IN VOTE TO SET UP NEGRO RIGHTS ORGANIZATION . . . Movement born with cheers of 1,000 Negroes in packed church here." The Birmingham News, June 6,1956, page 11.

Left: "Rev. Shuttlesworth . . . Leads Negro group."
Right: "Rev. G. W. McMurray . . . One dissenting."
The Birmingham News, June 6, 1956, page 11.

"As free and independent citizens of the United States of America and of the State of Alabama, we express publicly our determination to press persistently for freedom and democracy and the removal from our society any forms of second class citizenship."

# THE ORIGINAL DECLARATION OF PRINCIPLES

Mass Meeting On Civic Interest
Tuesday Night, June 5, 1956
Called by the Following Ministers: F. L. Shuttlesworth, N. H. Smith, Jr., T. L. Lane, R. L. Alford and G. E. Pruitt.

## PROCEEDINGS OF THE COMMITTEE ON RESOLUTIONS:

The Committee of 11 Ministers and Laymen met June 4th, 2:15 P.M. in the Smith and Gaston Funeral Chapel, 1600 5th Ave., N., to discuss plans, Principles, and Resolutions to be presented to the Mass Meeting. Rev. F. L. Shuttlesworth presided.

The discussion centered on the need of an organization to work in our Civic interest, and the State-Wide implications of such an Organization was mentioned by Rev. Alford. Also discussed, was the name by which such an Organization should be known. Next came the reading and discussion, and the adoption of a Declaration of Principles and Resolutions to be recommended to the Mass Meeting.

Discussion centered next on various committees, and the purported functioning of such Committees. Suggested was a Steering Committee (to be appointed in the Mass Meeting) to appoint other Committees for the organization. Each person pledged his and her all to the **Cause of Human Rights**, and spoke of the need now for our ambitions to be realized to the point of activity. The Committee made the following recommendations:

1. That this Mass Meeting form an Organization under the Name of "The Alabama Christian Movement for Human Rights."

2. That the following be adopted as a Declaration of Principles by the Organization:

(A) As free and independent Citizens of the United States of America, and of the State of Alabama, we express publicly our determination to press forward persistently for Freedom and Democracy, and the removal from our society any forms of Second Class Citizenship.

(B) We are not echoing the will or sentiments of Outsiders; but our own convictions and Will to be free, so help us God. We will not become Rabblerousers; but will be sober, firm, peaceful, and resolute, within the Framework of Goodwill.

(C) We Believe in our Courts and in Justice administered by our Courts; but we now point out to the Nation's conscience a strange paradox: One State District Court Judge can rule and immediately it is obeyed over the entire State — even if questioned or disagreed with; But even a unanimous Decision by 9 Judges of the U. S. Supreme Court (set up by the constitution to be the Highest and Final Court), and Rulings by Federal District Judges, representing the whole United States of America are not only questioned and disagreed with, but Openly Flaunted, Disregarded, and Totally Ignored.

(D) We Believe in State's Rights; but we believe that any first RIGHTS are HUMAN RIGHTS. And the first right of a State is to Protect Human Rights, and to guarantee to each of its Citizens the same Rights and Privileges.

(E) We heartily concur in and endorse the Rulings of the Federal Judiciary that **All** public Facilities belong to and should be open to All on the same and equal terms; and we Hope, Trust, and Pray that efforts to commence should be begun by Officials in the Spirit of Brotherhood and Goodwill; without the necessity of Lawsuits having to be filed.

(F) We most highly commend the activities of the Officials and Citizens everywhere for the efforts made for Civil Rights, and we thank God for them. But especially do we applaud Negroes in Montgomery, Ala., and Tallahassee, Fla., conducting themselves in the struggle so valiantly, and without rancor, hate, and smear, and above all without violence.

(G) As to Gradualism, we hold that it means to move forward, slowly maybe but surely; not vacillation, procrastination, or evasion. The hastily enacted laws and enflamed statements of Public Officials do not lead us to embrace Gradualism. We want a beginning **NOW! We have already waited 100 years!!**

(H) We Negroes shall never become enemies of the White People: We are all Americans; But America was born in the struggle for Freedom from Tyranny and Oppression. We shall never bomb any homes or lynch any persons; but we must, because of History and the future, march to Complete Freedom — with unbowed heads, praying hearts, and an unyielding determination. And we seek Guidance from our Heavenly Father; and from all men, Goodwill and understanding.

3. That a Steering Committee be appointed in this Mass Meeting to appoint the following other Committees: Finance, Education, Recreation, Transportation, Police Protection, Civic Rights, Jobs, Voting and Registration, Housing and Youth.

4. That this Mass Meeting go on record as unanimously supporting and applauding the efforts of Birmingham Negroes to form a Federal Loan Association in Birmingham.

5. That this Mass Meeting upon adjournment, will do so to meet Monday, June 11th, 7:00 o'clock, at the New Pilgrim Baptist Church, 903 South 6th Ave., Birmingham, Alabama.

**COMMITTEE:** Revs. F. L. Shuttlesworth, N. H. Smith, Jr., R. L. Alford, C. L. Vincent, C. H. George, Atty. Oscar W. Adams, Mrs. Lucinda Robey, C. J. Evans, G. C. Gissentanner, Mr. Lewis Willie, and others.

## Ministers Calling the June 5, 1956, Meeting

**Sardis Baptist Church** (*est. 1884, built 1920s, standing*) *ACMHR's First Meeting Site, June 5, 1956, 1240 Fourth Street North, Enon Ridge,* **Rev. Robert Louis Alford,** *Pastor (1950-1971), above right; Birmingham Public Library Department of Archives and Manuscripts Tax Assessor Files # 22-26-3-19-15; ACMHR Souvenir Booklet, 1958.*

*The Church then has to be the regulating force in society. No government, school, or organization can take the place of the organized Church in teaching spiritual, moral and ethical values and relating these to the lives of men. The Church is the leaven which Jesus said would make the whole lump rise. It is the salt that will season and give meaning to men's lives. Civil Rights is the Church's greatest challenge and greatest opportunity since the Middle Ages.* – Rev. Shuttlesworth, "The Church an Effective Witness In a Difficult Age."

**Bethel Baptist Church** (*est. 1904, 1926, standing*) *and adjacent Parsonage (1926-1956) right, 3191-3193 29th Avenue North, Collegeville,* **Rev. Fred Lee Shuttlesworth,** *Pastor (1953-1961), left.*

The Jefferson County tax assessor photograph, left bottom, the original Gothic-style church 13 years after its completion. Figurative stained glass windows, bright window trim and limestone coping accent the red brick church. The mortar is made with dark red, Birmingham iron ores. Birmingham Public Library Department of Archives and Manuscripts (BPLDAM) Jefferson County Tax Assessor Files (TAF) 22-13-4-33-1, January 4, 1939.

Bethel Baptist Church was established in the early-20th century as pig iron, foundry and railroad industries expanded on Birmingham's northern edge. By the 1950s, Bethel boasted a debt-free facility and a stalwart and growing membership with 400 to 500 attending Sunday services. Despite three bombings, ninety to ninety-five percent of members supported the Movement. Bethel became the platform on which Rev. Shuttlesworth stood to run the organization that marshaled the "folks" who would challenge segregation.

**New Hope Baptist Church**
*(est. 1892, 1912, demolished), 3421 Second Avenue North, Avondale,* **Rev. Herman Stone,** *Pastor (1946-1985), ACMHR Board. Located directly adjacent to the Sloss City Furnaces and the Avondale Mills, both large employers in the city center, New Hope's large congregation strongly supported ACMHR and hosted major mass meetings. BPLDAM-TAF 23-30-4-71, June 18, 1947; Stone portrait, New Hope Baptist Church, W.C. Motley Collection.*

**New Pilgrim Baptist Church**—*"The Church in America where people are taught that God is love, right is right, wrong is wrong, and all men are brothers!"—(est. 1900, 1945 & 1959, used as a day care center), 903 Sixth Avenue South, Southside, a large and active church with new facilities, a major ACMHR congregational supporter that hosted numerous meetings from 1956 to 1963 and led the "Freedom Walk" of 2,000 Sunday worshipers, May 5, 1963;* **Rev. Nelson H. Smith, Jr.,** *Pastor (1954-present), left, and ACMHR Secretary who with Rev. Shuttlesworth co-signed ACMHR releases;* **Rev. Charles Billups, Jr.,** *above, highly decorated veteran of two wars, Layman and Associate Pastor, ACMHR Ex. Board, BPLDAM-TAF 29-2-1-11-2, October 9, 1964. Pastors: ACMHR Souvenir Booklet, 1958. Rev. Billups participated in every major Birmingham demonstration.*

*These are grassroots pastors who really touched the people.* – Rev. Shuttlesworth, 1998.

**New Rising Star Baptist Church** *(est. 1958, built c. 1963), 3104 33rd Place, Collegeville,* **Rev. George E. Pruitt, Sr.,** *Pastor (1958-1986), left. BPLDAM-TAF 22-13-4-13-11, October 4, 1968; Portrait, Sadie Mae (Mrs. George) Pruitt, Queen Ester McArthur, Anetta Pruitt Moore, Jeannetta P. Woods and Rev. George E. Pruitt, Jr. A taxi driver and service station operator in the early years, Rev. Pruitt served on the Executive Board and often drove Rev. Shuttlesworth.*

## Other Key ACMHR Pastors and Incorporation Signers

Mount Olive Baptist Church (est. 1922, built by 1958, demolished), 6300 Third Avenue North, Woodlawn, **Rev. Edward M. Gardner,** Pastor (1949-present), left, and ACMHR Vice President (1956-1969) and President (1969-present). Rev. Gardner, together with Rev. Herman Stone, prepared programs for the regular Monday meetings. Often serving as the "warm up" preacher, Rev. Gardner conducted the business and gave a sermon or two. ACMHR Souvenir Booklets, 1958, 1965.

**Union Bethel Independent Methodist Church**—The Church With A Welcome To All—(est. 1952, built 1952), 1300 Sixth Avenue South, **Rev. T. L. Lane,** Pastor (1952-1962), ACMHR Souvenir Booklet, 1958. Portrait, Union Bethel Independent Methodist Church.

**Regular Missionary Baptist Church** (est. 1943, built 1945), 1205 Cahaba Street, East Birmingham, **Rev. C. H. George,** Pastor (1944-1972), BPLDAM-TAF 23-19-1-19-13, January 24, 1947; Pastor, Rev. Larry McCree, Jr.

**Zion Star Baptist Church** (est. 1913, demolished) far left, 2611 Fourth Avenue South, Southside, **Rev. James S. Phifer,** Pastor (1954-1963) left, ACMHR Annual Report, 1958. ACMHR Vice President, Rev. Phifer accompanied Rev. Shuttlesworth on legal challenges, including desegregation at Phillips High School in 1957. Rev. Phifer was jailed in 1962.

**First Metropolitan Baptist Church**—"The Church where the Gospel is preached with a Relevancy to Contemporary Problems"—(built 1930s, demolished), 2523 Fourth Avenue South, Southside, **Rev. Abraham Woods, Jr.**, Pastor (1954-1965) left; BPLDAM-TAF 23-31-3-25-1, January 20, 1939. Rev. Woods, a member of the Executive Board, and Johnnie L. Smith were responsible for securing churches for regular meetings.

**Oak Street Baptist Church** (est. 1916, built 1961) With View of Sloss-Sheffield's North Birmingham Cokeworks, left, 3224 Virginia Avenue, Collegeville, **Rev. C. L. Vincent** Pastor (1952-1963) left BPLDAM-TAF 22-13-1-19-7, 1-24-1947; Pastor photograph: Doris Gary.

# Articles of Incorporation

STATE OF ALABAMA
JEFFERSON COUNTY

CERTIFICATE OF INCORPORATION
OF
THE ALABAMA CHRISTIAN MOVEMENT
FOR HUMAN RIGHTS, INCORPORATED.

Filed 8-7-56
INC 105 Page 576

TO THE HONORABLE JUDGE OF THE PROBATE
COURT OF JEFFERSON COUNTY, ALABAMA

Under and by virture [sic] of the provisions of the Code of Alabama, 1940, Title 10, Chapter 10, and the supplement thereto, and the laws and Constitution of Alabama, the undersigned being desirous of organizing themselves together as a Non Profit Corporation, do hereby make and file this Declaration of Incorporation, pursuant to the provisions of said laws and become thereunder a body corporate, for the purpose herein after described, and do hereby declare and certify as follows, namely:

## ARTICLE I
### Name

The name of this Corporation shall be: The Alabama Christian Movement For Human Rights, Incorporated.

## ARTICLE II
### Location

The principle place of business and office of said corporation shall be located in Birmingham, Jefferson County, Alabama, until changed by appropriate action of the Board of Directors.

## ARTICLE III
### Duration

The duration of this Corporation shall be perpetual.

## ARTICLE IV
### Objects and Purposes

The objects and purposes for which the Corporation is formed are as follows:

(a) To use peaceful and lawful means in upholding the Constitution of the United States, and the Constitution of the State of Alabama;

(b) To press forward persistently for freedom and democracy, and the removal from our society of any form of second class citizenship;

(c) To preach and teach the principles of Christianity, embracing love, brotherhood, friendship, peace, fellowship, goodwill, and mutual understanding;

(d) To promote the economic, political, civic, and social development of all people;

(e) To work and associate with any organization which believes in the objects and purposes as set out in this certificate of incorporation;

(f) The Corporation shall have all the rights, power, privileges, and immunities as set out in the Code of Alabama, 1940, and all other laws applicable to Corporation organized therein, or as therein specifically set out or not, and all of which is hereby referred to and made a part hereof as though fully set out herein.

## ARTICLE V
### Non-Pecuniary

This Corporation shall not issue shares of stock and it is not organized for any pecuniary purposes.

## ARTICLE VI
### Limited Liability

The members of the Corporation shall not be liable for any of the Corporate debts or obligations, nor for any acts of the Corporation which may result in liability to it.

## ARTICLE VII
### Membership

Any person who is in accord with the objects and purposes of this corporation may become a member. Membership in the Corporation shall not be divided into classes.

## ARTICLE VIII
### Address of Initial Registered Office and Agent

The address of the initial registered office of the Corporation is 3191 North 29th Avenue, Birmingham, Alabama; and the name of the initial registered agent at said address: Reverend F. L. Shuttlesworth.

## ARTICLE IX
### Board of Directors

The number of directors constituting the initial Board of Directors is twelve, and the names and addresses of the persons who are to serve as initial directors are:

| | |
|---|---|
| F. L. Shuttlesworth | R. L. Alford |
| F. Ellis Bell | N. H. Smith, Jr |
| Mrs. Lucinda B. Robey | W. E. Shortridge |
| C. H. George | T. L. Lane |
| Johnnie L. Smith | Abraham Woods, Jr. |
| Charlie Watson | Herman Stone |

## ARTICLE X

In the event of the dissolution of this Corporation, or in the event it shall cease to carry out the objects and purposes set forth, all the business, property and assets of the Corporation shall go and be distributed to such non-profit charitable Corporations or associations, as may be selected by the Board of Directors of this Corporation so that the business properties and assets of this Corporation shall, in that event, be used for and devoted to continue the purposes set out in this Article of Incorporation by some other non-profit Corporation or association, and in no event shall any of the assets or property of this Corporation, or the proceeds of any of said assets or property, in the event of dissolution, thereof, go or be distributed to members either for the reimbursement of any sum subscribed, donated, or contributed by such member; it being intent that in the event of the dissolution of this Corporation, or upon it ceasing to carry out the objects and purposes herein set forth, the property and assets then owned by the Corporation shall be devoted to the carrying on of the present purposes of this Corporation by some other non-profit charitable organization or association as the Board of Directors shall determine and direct.

IN TESTIMONY WHEREOF, the said persons who are incorporators of The Alabama Christian Movement For Human Rights Incorporated, severally hereunto sign and subscribe their names and file the same for record in the office of the Judge of the Probate Court of Jefferson, County, Alabama, and request that the Judge of the Probate Court of Jefferson County record hereon a certificate of registration showing the book and page wherein recorded for the purpose of protecting the formation of this corporation in manner and form provided by the law, on this the 16th day of August, 1956.

F. L. Shuttlesworth

R. L. Alford

F. Ellis Bell

N. H. Smith, Jr.

Mrs. Lucinda B. Robey

W. E. Shortridge

C. H. George

T. L. Lane

Johnnie L. Smith

(Rev.) Abraham Woods, Jr.

Charlie Watson

Herman Stone

## Seeking Jobs

During the seven and one-half years before the demonstrations of 1963, ACMHR moved by petition and lawsuit against all areas of segregation in Birmingham. The first challengers – George Johnson and Clyde Jones – tried to take civil service examinations to apply for positions as police. After the Personnel Board refused to allow them to take these exams, ACMHR filed suit.

## Terrorism Builds Solidarity

*God saved the Reverend to lead the fight!* – Unidentified woman in the crowd gathered outside the bombed-out parsonage as Rev. Shuttlesworth emerged, unharmed, from the debris, December 25, 1958.

*If God could save me through this, then I'm gonna stay here and clear this up. . . . I wasn't saved to run.* – Rev. Shuttlesworth, to Howell Raines, *My Soul Is Rested*, 1977.

*That act of violence eliminated all fear that had a grip on black people, for so long, in the City of Birmingham and encouraged their resolve to seek their rights under American law.* – Reuben Davis, Bethel Church Member, Jefferson County Commissioner (1987-1991), 1995.

# A Bomb for Christmas, Bethel Baptist Church

*Bethel Parsonage With Policemen and Cars in Foreground, December 25, 1956, Reuben Davis Collection, Birmingham. The night before the protest of the segregation of public transportation, 16 sticks of dynamite exploded in the space between the Bethel Church and its parsonage. The residence, in which Shuttlesworth and a church deacon who was guarding him were sitting at the time of the blast, collapsed.*

Efforts to intimidate ACMHR members from riding the buses were not only unsuccessful but, indeed, proved the major event that catapulted Rev. Shuttlesworth into messianic leadership. The intimidation efforts galvanized black support for the Movement.

*Shuttlesworth's Christmas present convinced both him and his followers that God had truly singled him out for leadership.* – Andrew M. Manis, Religious Historian and Rev. Shuttlesworth's biographer, *"A Fire You Can't Put Out," The Civil Rights Life of the Birmingham's Fred Shuttlesworth*, 1999.

# Fight for Freedom on Buses

In December of 1956, the U. S. Supreme Court upheld a lower court ruling that segregation on buses in Montgomery was unconstitutional. ACMHR countered by asking the Birmingham City Commission to voluntarily rescind local bus segregation laws. The Commission refused. Despite the Christmas night bombing of his home, the next day, undaunted and unafraid, Rev. Shuttlesworth led more than 300 Negroes in a mass violation of the bus law. Twenty-two people were arrested and fined in City Court. ACMHR filed suit in Federal Court.

*"IN WHITE SECTION OF BUS (right above), Negroes of Birmingham ignore the Jim Crow sign as they invite arrest during a two-day demonstration by sitting in front seats that hitherto had been forbidden to them." Robert Adams,* The Birmingham News, *photograph and caption published in* Life Magazine, *January 7, 1957.*

*"HAPPY MARTYRS (right below), some of 22 arrested in the Birmingham demonstration and freed on $100 bail, are praised by Rev. Mr. Shuttlesworth (leaning on pulpit, in light coat) at a church antisegregation meeting."* Montgomery Advertiser, *photograph and caption published in* Life Magazine, *January 7, 1957, page 35, possibly St James Baptist Church.*

*"NEGROES MEET — Part of the overflow crowd at St. Paul Methodist Church last night is shown above. They were told that a Federal injunction will be asked as a result of bus segregation arrests made yesterday during the mass bus-riding moves by Negroes."* Birmingham Post-Herald, *December 27, 1958, page 2.*

## Southern Christian Leadership Conference Organized

Alabama-based pastors, including Rev. Martin Luther King, Jr., Rev. Ralph Abernathy, Rev. Joseph Lowery and Rev. Fred Shuttlesworth, led this new "organization of organizations." SCLC would grow to be a large corporation with a network of more than 85 local civil rights affiliates. ACMHR would be a strong local center and a model for others across the nation. Rev. Shuttlesworth would serve as Secretary from the founding in 1957 until 1969.

### MARCH 6, 1957

## Freedom on Interstate Transportation. The Terminal Station

On December 22, 1956, police had arrested two prominent Blacks, Carl and Alexenia Baldwin, for refusing to move to the "colored" section of the Birmingham Terminal (railroad) station. The ACMHR sponsored their legal fight. Failing to win, Rev. Shuttlesworth and his wife Ruby personally challenged segregated accommodations at the station. The Interstate Commerce Commission had banned segregation among interstate passengers. Vigilante violence ensued after Lamar Weaver, a white minister, sat down and waited for the Atlanta train with the Shuttlesworths. Weaver and his convertible were stoned. Police at the scene did not provide him support. The Shuttlesworths traveled to Atlanta in the white section of the train.

### MAY 17, 1957

## *The Social Gospel: The New Negro Church*

*Excerpts: "The New Negro Church," Speech by Rev. Fred Shuttlesworth, one of four "Southern Freedom Fighters," Prayer Pilgrimage, Washington, D. C.*

In this speech delivered to a major gathering of Negro leaders, Rev. Shuttlesworth states the role of the church in daily affairs. A proponent of the social gospel, Shuttlesworth interprets Christianity as a spirit of brotherhood revealed in social ethics. The minister applies his teaching and leadership abilities to issues of public morality, bringing God's love and justice to all men:

*But a new voice is arising all over now — the voice of the church of a living and ruling God, unafraid, uncompromising, and unceasing. Led by her ministers, she cries out that all men are brothers, and that justice and mercy must flow as the waters. The Negro Church is taking the lead, and thank God, some in the White Church are at last pleading for justice and reason. We have arisen to walk with destiny, and we shall march till victory is won. Not a victory for Negroes, but a victory for America, for right, for righteousness. No man can make us hate; and no men can make us afraid. We know that the struggle will be hard and costly; some of us indeed may die; but let our trials and death — if come they must — be one more sacred installment on this American heritage for freedom; and let History and they that come behind us, rejoice that we arose in strength, armed only with the weapon of Love, and stood where men stood, and removed from American society this cancerous infection of Segregation and 2nd class citizenship.*

# *A Faith for Difficult Times*

### Excerpts: Rev. Shuttlesworth's Annual Report to the ACMHR

But they reckoned without the power of Almighty God, or forgot to remember that Faith works its best miracles under difficult and critical circumstances. For we arose up that historic night to keep our date with destiny. We stood together as one man pledging each to the other our lives, our fortunes, our sacred honor. With massive voice from unafraid hearts, we cried out "Give us liberty or give us death." We possessed that night a "faith that would not shrink, though pressed by every foe."

We stood up like men of faith, with love in our hearts, but with determination in our breasts not only to defy and challenge Segregation practices and customs, but also to say to the "Uncle Toms" of yesterday, "get behind us Satan, for you are offensive to us. You have kept us behind long enough. No longer do we need you to procrastinate and receive "pats" and "handouts." Find your crack and hide, for Negroes from henceforth will follow a leadership that will lead to the mountain top. Crumbs will no longer sustain us; we must have part of the loaf that is democracy. Some became angry and envious, and the politicians raved; but together we have marched for a whole year. Some felt that this was just another "stunt" by eager and misguided Negroes, and that it would - as had many things in the past - blow over in a fortnight. It was felt that "they're hot now but they'll cool off afterwhile."

But God was speaking to us and through us, and tonight the "stunt" is still going strong; stronger than ever before. For in spite of the slander we have withstood, the threats that we have heard, and the violence we have sustained, I am sure, positively sure, that nothing shall stop us until we cross the Segregation river and tread the shores in our day of unrestricted freedom . . .

And so tonight, we reaffirm our Faith in the American Democracy, and pledge our continued resistance to Segregation and Discrimination. We must never retreat from this position no matter what the cost. There must be one law for all or there will be no peace. We are called upon by God to stand now like men. Therefore be strong, and of good courage . . . and let us play the men for our people . . . and the Lord do that which seemeth Him good. *2nd Samuel 10:12.* . . .

Let us go on knowing in our hearts that we hate no one, nor will we harm anyone. Let us persevere through this midnight of terror and madness, so that the American children of the Future will not have to undergo these ordeals: and thus will rise up and call us blessed.

# The Birmingham News

The Braves hanging on despite pitching troubles! See Page 17.

OTHER PAGES:

| | Page | | Page |
|---|---|---|---|
| Social | 10 | Comics | 21 |
| Editorials | 14 | Radio-TV | 22 |
| Crossword | 16 | Amusements | 24 |
| Sports | 17 | Bridge | 26 |

BIRMINGHAM AND VICINITY: Partly cloudy and cool tonight, Tuesday, partly cloudy and warmer with occasional showers, mostly in the afternoon. High today, 78. Low tonight, 62. High Tuesday, 80.

*(Furnished by U. S. Weather Bureau)*

**70TH YEAR—NO. 154** · 30 Pages · BIRMINGHAM, ALA., MONDAY, SEPTEMBER 9, 1957 · ★ · PRICE: 5 CENTS

### Rev. Shuttlesworth attacked in integration try—

# Negro beaten at Phillips High
# Whites eject Arkansas Negroes

## N. Little Rock students oust six at school

LITTLE ROCK, Ark., Sept. 9—(AP)—Shouting white students grabbed six Negro youths who tried to enter North Little Rock High School today and shoved them off the campus despite the efforts of the superintendent to escort them into the building.

It was the first actual physical clash between whites and Negroes and marked a new front of tension in the worsening race situation in the Little Rock area.

North Little Rock is an adjacent municipality of 50,000 just across the Arkansas River from here. The new school term started today, a week later than in Little Rock.

THE SIX NEGRO boys advanced toward the front entrance of the school where they were met by a group of white boys with fists doubled. The whites hustled the Negroes away from the school. The Negro boys were not hurt.

Supt. F. B. Wright came to the scene and gestured for the

**THE REV. F. L. SHUTLESWORTH SHOWN AS HE WAS KNOCKED TO STREET OUTSIDE SCHOOL**
... A lone policeman was pushed aside by the crowd when the Negro drove up to the school.

*WAPI-TV Newsreel picture*

## Minister had sought entry of children

A Negro integration leader was beaten by a group of white men when he tried to enter his daughter and other Negro students at Phillips High School this morning.

Three white men were arrested at the scene and held for questioning.

Still undergoing treatment at University Hospital, the Rev. F. L. Shuttlesworth said another attempt will be made Tuesday to enroll Negro students at Phillips "whether they kill us or not . . ."

Police said this afternoon that school officials had been advised that Negro students would be presented for enrollment at Woodlawn High School "before noon tomorrow."

The Rev. F. L. Shuttlesworth, 3232 29th-av, n, who petitioned the Birmingham School Board to enter his daughter at Phillips

Just a week after U. S. Marshals protected students at Central High School in Little Rock, Arkansas, Rev. Shuttlesworth attempted to enroll his daughters in Birmingham's major high school and met with mob violence. The mob was apparently intent on killing or seriously injuring Shuttlesworth. Despite significant injuries, the ACMHR leader appeared at a mass meeting that evening to preach non-violence, quell potential rioting and raise funds for the Movement. ACMHR later files suit challenging Alabama's school segregation laws.

*In the photograph (right), a basket is passed to collect donations from latecomers to the Mass Meeting held, the night of the Phillips incident, at New Hope Baptist Church in Avondale.*

ACMHR raises its funds to underwrite suits, such as the school case resulting from this day's challenge, court costs, bonds and fees through offerings, such as this one. A typical mass meeting offering brings in $200 to $300. Dollar by dollar, ACMHR locally sustains its fight against segregation in Birmingham. *Birmingham Post-Herald*, September 10, 1957, page 6.

*"Woodlawn Students Demonstrate Against Integration . . . Students warned to have proper excuses or face expulsion."*
The Birmingham News, September 10, 1957, page 1

# There are No Short Cuts

Cartoon by Harper, The Birmingham News, September 11, 1957, page 4.

*"Students Evacuate Phillips After Anonymous Bomb Threat . . . Some 1850 left the building scene of violence yesterday."* The Birmingham News, September 10, 1957, page 1.

# Raw Violence

Editorial reprinted from the *Birmingham World,* Sept. 18, 1957, Page 6.

Recent episodes of violence in Birmingham should impel law enforcement and the other community leaders to make a reappraisal of the local situation, a program of preventive violence is necessary.

A few days ago, the Rev. F. L. Shuttlesworth was ganged, cornered and beaten at a public high school by those who sought to forcibly prevent him from applying for enrollment of his children in the nearest school. Obstructionists were on hand to stop him. Whatever judgement one might hold with reference to his methods, motives, and timing, no one has said, or could say, he was violent or forcing his way.

He selected one of the ways by which those interested in bringing the local law in line with the highest law might use. The principal of the school was competent to handle the situation. Certainly, the constituted representatives of public law knew how to deal with it. Such is never the work of the mob. Never is a mob or those of similar methods the proper ones to handle such matters.

Violence is no answer to change. Violence can only set back our community and help to build a fire under those customs which are tottering under the cosmic power of change. Violence is the mother of anarchy.

# "The Movement is Moving"

## Message From Our President, June 1958

The greatest issue in human affairs today is that of Freedom: simple justice, fair play, equality of human beings irrespective of color, and the sharing of opportunities — socially, economically, and politically. The fact that the struggle is in full force around the world is assurance enough that it is ordered by Divine Decree; for this is still my God's world. Oppressed people throughout the Continents and the Islands of the Seas are rising up and calling for their God-given Rights. Colonialism, imperialism, segregation and discrimination, economic exploitation, taxation without representation, and government without participation are all under sustained attack. "I like to think of this world wide revolution as being "A Divine Struggle for the exaltation of the human race."

## *Progress In Spite of Circumstances*

Excerpts: Rev. Shuttlesworth's *Annual Report to the ACMHR*

Who would dare disturb this vicious giant? Who would challenge this way of life which has sent justice to take an extended holiday, and when angry, knows not mercy? Who would tackle such a foe as segregation, which has strangled state courts, taken over executive functions, and so confused lawmakers' minds that keeping segregation is now more important than either saving the prestige of America or going to Heaven. Small wonder this organization has been branded as "stirring up trouble!" Small wonder that men of trembling heart and nervous frames have called us "fools." . . .

This is a religious crusade, a fight between light and darkness, right and wrong, good and evil, fair play versus tyranny. We are assured of victory because we are using weapons of spiritual warfare. Against the racist's hate and scorn we are using the love of Christ, against his oppressive and abusive acts we are using the weapon of Prayer on whose mystic wings we sweep into the presence of God to lay out our troubles. Thus we are never tempted to hate White people or to return them evil for evil. This organization frowns on violence—therefore no Negro must allow himself to become so angry that he will disgrace the cause for which we fight and suffer. . . .

Oh! Mother America, where is thy solace for thy children's ills? Where is the freedom you so freely offer others? Where is your soul that you allow liberty to be trodden in the dust? Why kill defenseless Negroes who only ask freedom while coddling in your arms those who more than once have gleefully spilled your blood on foreign soil? . . .

**Executive Board and Advisory Committee:** *Standing, front row, left to right: Mr. J. J. Ryles, Mrs. Georgia Price, Rev. H. Stone, Mrs. Daisy Jeffries, Mr. E. H. Murphy, Mr. H. N. Guinn, Mrs. Lola Hendricks, Mrs. Altha Stallworth, Mr. James Armstrong, Rev. G. E. Pruitt, Mrs. Josephine Jones. Second row: Rev. J. A. Hayes, Mrs. Rella Williams, Mrs. Lucinda Brown Robey\*, Mr. W. E. Shortridge\*, (seated), Rev. Abraham Woods, Jr., Mrs. Myrtice Dowdell, Rev. J. S. Phifer, Rev. N. H. Smith, Jr.\*, Rev. F. L. Shuttlesworth\*, Rev. Charles Billups, Mrs. Dester Brooks, Rev. Edward Gardner\*, Rev. L. J. Rogers, and Mr. George Price (\*Indicates Executive Officer), ACMHR Souvenir Booklet, 1958.*

## *"People who walked with us through the storm."* – FLS/98

**The First Membership Committee:** *Standing, left to right: Mr. Charles Billups, Mrs. Georgia Price, Mr. J. L. Colbert, Mrs. Marie Wilson, and Mr. William Parker. Seated, left to right: Mrs. Dorothy Morris, Mrs. Daisy Jeffries, Mrs. Lena Thomas, Mrs. Myrtis Dowdell. ACMHR Souvenir Booklet, 1958.*

# Inspirational Music

In July, 1960, ACMHR leaders W. E. Shortridge and Georgia Price organized the Movement Choir. Under the direction of 18-year-old composer, Carlton Reese, the choir's repetoire combined traditional hymns and gospel music. Favorites included: "Ain't Gonna Let Nobody Turn Me Around," "We've Got A Job," "Ninety-Nine Percent Won't Do" and "Freedom Is Just Ahead!" The choir sang regularly at meetings, heightening their intensity.

*Singing provided inspiration, a way of praising God and spiritual uplift.* — Doris Gary, ACMHR Member, Collegeville, 1998.

*The music of the Birmingham Movement reflected its top-drawer level of organization and strategy.* — Bernice Reagon, *Songs of the Civil Rights Movement.*

*ACMHR Choir. Officers: Carlton Reese, Organist and Director, Andrew B. Sneed, Jr., Pianist, Lincoln Hendricks, President; Lola Hendricks Collection.*

# Women Leaders

**Lola Hendricks**
*Corresponding Secretary, 1956-1963*

**Julia Rainge**
*Corresponding Secretary*

**Georgia Price**
*Executive Committee & Officer*

**Lucinda Brown Robey,**
*Officer & Youth Division Directrice*

**Ruby Shuttlesworth**
*Youth Division Directrice*

These ladies were among the leaders who coordinated ACMHR efforts. Mrs. Price served on the Executive Committee and headed up many a special project. Mrs. Hendricks served as liaison to SCLC coordinator Wyatt Tee Walker during the joint SCLC-ACMHR campaign of spring 1963. Photographs: *ACMHR Souvenir Booklets* and Doris Gary.

*"Shuttlesworth would call down from New York, and by the time he got here, we'd have the church full."* — Lola Hendricks, 1998.

Trained as a nurse, Ruby Shuttlesworth helped organize ACMHR youth activities and accompanied her husband on direct action challenges. Her home was destroyed by a bomb in 1956. She was stabbed in the hip by a mobster at Phillips High School in 1957, and her husband and children were arrested in desegregation efforts. Mrs. Shuttlesworth strongly supported the Movement.

# "Today's Church Working for Tomorrow's World"
## Bethel Baptist Church

*WORSHIP FURNISHINGS*

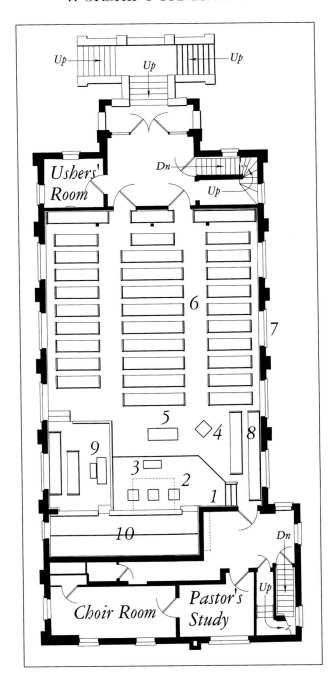

*MOVEMENT MEETING SETUP*

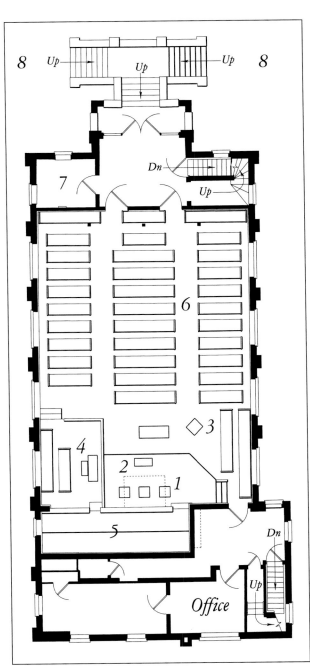

WORSHIP FURNISHINGS, 1960s
1. Church Covenant (framed, 1996).
2. Pulpit Chairs (extant, 1996), center chair for pastor, flanking chairs for visiting clergy.
3. Pulpit on Raised Stage (pulpit on exhibit at Birmingham Civil Rights Institute, 1996).
4. Clerk's Table (extant, 1996).
5. Sacramental Table (Usher's Room, 1996).
6. Walnut Benches (used in basement and other rooms, 1996) Sanctuary was used for services and meetings, but not for Sunday School.
7. Figured Stained Glass Windows, installed 1926 (destroyed by 1956 bombing).
8. Deacon and Trustee Pews.
9. Richmond Piano (in storage, 1996).
10. Choir Stand (folding wooden chairs for 15 to 30 persons).

MOVEMENT MEETING SETUP, 1960s
1. Chairs for Alabama Christian Movement for Human Rights (ACMHR) Leaders and Guest Speakers.
2. Pulpit. A public address system is installed to improve sound for the mass meetings.
3. Table for ACMHR Treasurer, William. E. Shortridge.
4. Electronic Organ (purchased late 1950s or early 1960s).
5. Choir (15 or 20 people).
6. Meeting were attended by 450 to 600 people, including police officers. Police also drove by outside during proceedings.
7. Guard or Look-Out Room.
8. Volunteer Guards, stationed outside church.

*Organization of Space for Worship and for ACMHR Meetings, Bethel Baptist Church, Historic American Engineering Record–National Park Service Birmingham Industrial District Project, ink on mylar drawing by Richard Anderson and Marjorie White, 1996.*

# "Bethel was the Movement and the Movement was the Church"

The Bethel Baptist Church provided its facilities including meeting spaces and offices, rent and utilities free to ACMHR. The Bethel sanctuary hosted many mass meetings. Bethel also served as the ACMHR headquarters until 1961. The church paid not only a pastor's salary to Rev. Shuttlesworth and provided him with a residence and volunteer guards, but also paid the church secretary's salary, while allowing her to work on Movement business. Bethel members strongly supported the Movement.

*We could always go to Bethel. Her doors were open.*
– Rev. Shuttlesworth, 1998.

## Volunteer Guards

After the 1956 bombing, Bethel members (and later ACMHR volunteer guards) provided protection for the Bethel Church, for Rev. Shuttlesworth and for the homes of those persons who participated in school integration cases. Guards also protected host churches during the mass meetings.

*ACMHR Guards: George Walker and James Armstrong ("the lead men"), Charlie Brooks, Mrs. Dester Brooks, Walter Brown, Julius Clark, Sr., Robert Coar, Lige Dawson, Mrs. Minnie Eaton, George Forrest, Carter Gaston, Will Hall, Charlie Hatcher, Jake Head, Jim Hendricks, Joe Hendricks, Lincoln Hendricks, John Hullett, Colonel Stone Johnson, Ruben Mason, Georgia Price (Coordinator), James Pullom, Ollie Rainge, Mack E. Roberson, Mrs. Lucinda Brown Robey, James Russell, Frank L. Seay, John Tolbert, Jr., Randolph Thomas, and N. B. Wooding, Jr.*

## Sustaining the Legal Fight

During ACMHR's first three years, the organization spent $40,429 of the $53,000 they raised on court costs, with $24,000 going to black attorneys. Donations at the mass meetings and fees for speaking engagements financed these court costs, bonds and other fees.

*The basis of support was poor people, not the middle class or white sympathizers . . . people giving their money.*
– Rev. Shuttlesworth, 1998.

Attorneys active in ACMHR cases included Arthur D. Shores, Bus Case; Orzell Billingsley, Jr., and Oscar Adams, Jr., Police Case; Demetrius Newton, Initial Terminal Station Case; Ernest D. Jackson, Sr., Jacksonville, Fla., School Case.

# "Latest Night of Terror"
## Bethel Bombed Again

*Pulpit, Bethel Baptist Church, Looking Through Shattered Windows, 1958, Reuben Davis Collection, Birmingham.*

During 1958, bombings increase across the city. On April 28, fifty-four sticks of dynamite fail to explode at Temple Beth-El on Highland Avenue. This bomb attempt is subsequently linked to anti-Semitic white supremacist activity in other Southern cities. Members of the Jewish community pressure City Hall regarding appropriate protection.

At the same time, Rev. Shuttlesworth and ACMHR petition for black policemen. On the night of June 2, 1958, volunteer guards diffuse a bomb which would have destroyed the Bethel church had it fully exploded.

*Pulpit and Bible, Bethel Baptist Church, Reuben Davis Collection, Birmingham.*

*They were determined to get rid of the church. They wanted to destroy my base. Had the guards not moved the bomb, it would have torn the walls down.* – Rev. Shuttlesworth, 1998.

*East Facade, Bethel Baptist Church with members gathered to review impact of bombing, June 1958. The arched metal-frame windows were shattered by the glass. The brick infill at the top of these windows (with light-colored motar) reflects the repairs that had been made following the destruction of the original, figurative stained-glass windows in the 1956 bombing. While Bethel Church guards, Will Hall and Col. Stone Johnson, partly diffused the bomb, shards remain in the brickwork along this facade. The bomb was placed so as to implode the church. Reuben Davis Collection, Birmingham.*

# "Ordinary people: no class, low class and becoming some class"

*Monday Movement Meeting, June 23,1958, East Thomas Baptist Church, Rev. J. A. Hayes, Pastor, ACMHR Souvenir Booklet, 1958.*

*The Organization met every Monday night in different churches all over the city. The mass meetings were full of religious fervor and were so well attended by the faithful, 300 to 400 of whom attended regularly each Monday.* – Rev. Shuttlesworth, 1998.

*This was not a ministerial association. It was people more than pastors. Pastors and members of individual churches welcomed the ministerial-led movement. People who attended the mass meetings put pressure on their pastors to host meetings. . . . To be a meeting church was to invite terror from the police and the Klan.* — Rev. Shuttlesworth, 1998.

# *Movement Meeting Churches*

By 1958, ACMHR's network of 55 working-class churches extends across the industrial city. Most churches are located adjacent to industrial plants where many ACMHR members work. With 300 to 400 "regulars" attending mass meetings every Monday night, small churches could be used only occasionally. At these sites, meetings served to diversify the core support and educate host church members in the Movement's mission.

Of the 55 Birmingham area churches hosting mass meetings in the early years of the Movement, only New Pilgrim Baptist, New Hope Baptist, St. James Baptist, St. Luke A.M. E., Seventeenth Street A.O.H. Church of God, First Baptist Church of Ensley and Thirty-Second Street Baptist Church — all with capacities of 600 to 900 — could hold the crowds that came in times of testing of segregation laws and after ACMHR's legal successes of the early 1960s gave hope to the cause.

This list of Movement Meeting Churches includes the 1963 church name, address and city neighborhood. In 1998, all Movement church congregations remain. Several have new names (indicated in the list in parentheses) and new campuses. Those churches with an asterisk * still use their Movement-era churches for worship, Sunday school or day care. Those structures indicated with a † now serve other congregations.

For a more complete listing of Movement Meeting churches and photographic credits, see page 80-82. As photographers working for the Jefferson County tax assessor made most photographs shown here, the tax assessor record number appears in many images. A map of all churches accompanies this publication.

**NORTH BIRMINGHAM**
* 1. **Bethel Baptist Church,** 3191 29th Ave. N.
* 2. **Christian Valley Baptist Church,** 3104 33rd Terrace N.

* 3. **First Baptist Church, Hooper City,** 468 37th Ct. W.
* 4. **Hopewell Baptist Church,** 2315 6th Ave. N., ACIPCO

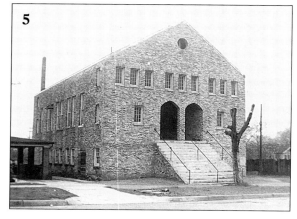

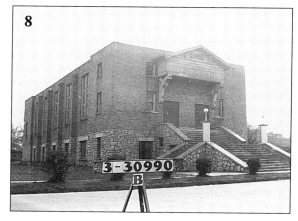

5. **Lily Grove Baptist Church,**
   1015 3rd St. N., Druid Hills

\* 6. **New Rising Star Baptist Church,**
   3104 33rd Pl. N., Collegeville

7. **New Salem Baptist Church,** 1632 Sixth St. N.
   ACIPCO

\* 8. **St. Luke A.M.E. Church,** 2803 21st Ave. N.

\* 9. **Oak Street Baptist Church,**
   3224 Virginia Ave., Collegeville

\* 10. **Shady Grove Baptist Church,**
   3444 31st Way N., Collegeville

\* 11. **Twenty-Second Avenue Baptist Church,**
   2614 22nd Ave. N.

NORTHSIDE

\* 12. **Galilee Baptist Church,** 1013 23rd St. N.

13. **Macedonia Seventeenth Street Baptist
    Church,** 922 17th St. N.

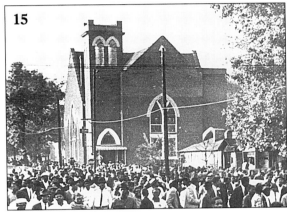

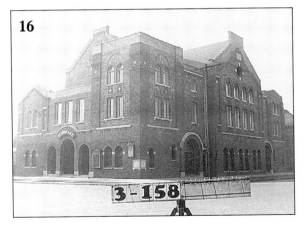

* 14. (Sixth Street) Peace Baptist Church, 302 Sixth St. N.

15. St. James Baptist Church, 1100 Sixth Ave. N.

16. St. John A.M.E. Church, 1400 Seventh Ave. N.

* 17. St. Paul (United) Methodist Church, 1500 Sixth Ave. N.

18. Seventeenth Street A.O.H. Church, 630 17th St. N.

† 19. Sixth Avenue Zion Hill Baptist Church, 1414 Sixth Ave. N.

20. Tabernacle Baptist Church, 1013 25th St. N.

ENSLEY

* 21. Abyssinia Baptist Church, 1501 Ave. L

* 22. Bethel A.M.E. Church, 1524 Ave. D

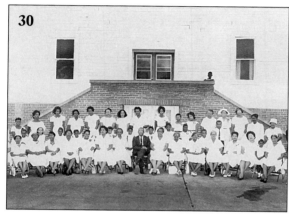

23. **First Baptist Church, Ensley,** 1534 19th St.

† 24. **Metropolitan C.M.E. Church,** 1733 18th St.

∗ 25. **Mt. Ararat Baptist Church,** 1920 Slayden Ave.

26. **St. Paul C.M.E. Church,** 400 Circle St., Docena

**EASTERN AREA: AVONDALE, WOODLAWN, EAST BIRMINGHAM, KINGSTON**

∗ 27. **First Baptist Church, Kingston,** 4600 9th Ave. N., Kingston

28. **First Baptist Church, Woodlawn,** 301 62nd St. S, Woodlawn

29. **Forty-Sixth Street Baptist Church,** 1532 Cahaba St., East Birmingham

30. **Groveland Baptist Church,** 452 66th St. N., Woodlawn

31. **Jackson Street Baptist Church,** 230 63rd St. S, Woodlawn

\* **32. Metropolitan Community Church,**
335 64th St. South, Woodlawn

**33. Mt. Olive Baptist Church,**
6300 Third Ave. N., Woodlawn

**34. New Hope Baptist Church,**
3421 Second Ave. N., Avondale

**35. Regular (St. Matthew) Missionary Baptist Church,** 1205 Cahaba St., East Birmingham

\* **36. St. Luke A.M.E. Zion Church,**
3937 12th Ave. N., East Birmingham

\* **37. Zion Spring Baptist Church,** 528 41st St.

**SMITHFIELD & EAST THOMAS**

\* **38. First Ebenezer Baptist Church,**
420 Graymont Ave. W.

\* **39. Sardis Baptist Church,** 1240 Fourth St. N.

**40. St. Paul A.M.E. Church,** 300 4th Ct. N.

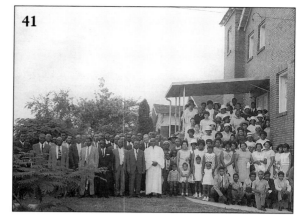

\* **41. First Baptist Church, East Thomas,** 419 11th Ct. W.

**SOUTHSIDE**

\* **42. East End Baptist Church,** 2609 Sixth Ave. S.

43. **First Metropolitan Baptist Church,** 2523 Fourth Ave. S.

\* **44. New Pilgrim Baptist Church,** 903 Sixth Ave. S.

\* **45. South Elyton Baptist Church,** 102 First St. S.

† **46. Thirty-Second Street Baptist Church,** 518 32nd St. S.

47. **Union Bethel Independent Methodist Church,** 1300 Sixth Ave. S.

48. **Zion Star Baptist Church,** 2611 Fourth Ave. S.

**POWDERLY, WEST END**

\* **49. St. John Baptist Church,** 1280 AL 150, 1280 AL 150, Powderly

# Police Surveillance of ACMHR Meetings Begins

Police Commissioner Theopholis Eugene "Bull" Connor regularly assigned two or more detectives to sit in the mass meetings. Using radio communications, police transcribed proceedings, filing reports of which 169 remain for the period January 1961 to December 1963. These reports are included in the Bull Connor papers at the Birmingham Public Library Department of Archives and Manuscripts.

*The police became more friendly as we went on. Some became our friends. They understood the Movement. . . .When the police would go there (to the ACMHR meetings) and be nice and get religion, Bull (Connor) would move them.* – Col. Stone Johnson, 1998.

*The Movement met every Monday night after June 5, 1956, and when any trouble or testing would arise, we met every night. The police didn't get them all. Police reports do not necessarily list all the meetings and all the churches.* — Rev. Shuttlesworth, 1998.

\* 50. **West End Hills Baptist Church,**
　　1700 19th Place SW

**BESSEMER & FAIRFIELD**
\* 51. **Canaan (Missionary) Baptist Church,**
　　824 15th St. N.
\* 52. **New Bethlehem Baptist Church,**
　　1730 Eleventh Ave. N.

53. **Pleasant Grove Baptist Church,**
　　14-37th Street, Fairfield
\* 54. **Starlight Baptist Church,**
　　1280 AL 150, Muscoda
55. **St. Peters Primitive Baptist Church,**
　　2115 Fourth Ave. N. (bricked in 1963)

# BIRMINGHAM: Integration's Hottest Crucible

Reprinted from *TIME,* December 15, 1958, Page 16.

BIRMINGHAM, ALA., *(pop. 360,150). Most concentrated heavy-industry city in Deep South, steel mills, iron foundries, etc., set up 1871 in midst of Jones Valley iron ore, coal, limestone; now centers around Tennessee Coal & Iron Division of U.S. Steel Corp. with 25,000 employees, also diversifies into 720 firms, e.g., Hayes Aircraft Corp., which turn out 3,250 products. Ample cheap labor force: rural white immigrants, Negroes. Negro population: 38.9%, with rising living standards, though only 21.1% of Negro families make upwards of $4,000 a year against 77.2% of whites. Tourist attraction: Vulcan, 55-ft. monument on top of 120-ft. pedestal on Red Mountain to god of metalwork.*

VULCAN'S city burned with resentment last week as it waited for U.S. Attorney General William P. Rogers to make good on his promise to call the federal grand jury to investigate a possible violation of civil rights by Birmingham's police force. Six weeks ago, Birmingham's cops arrested three Negro ministers from Montgomery who were caught talking with local Negro leaders about a possible bus boycott, charged them with vagrancy. Said Birmingham's police chief, Eugene Connor, who refused even to discuss the case with FBI agents: "I haven't got any damn apology to the FBI or anybody else. Maybe I just didn't tell the FBI what Rogers wanted me to tell them. Maybe that's why that jackass is yapping his brains out."

Bull Connor is a big voice in Birmingham, where a smelter economy, stamped onto Alabama's rural culture, makes a melting pot of raw men as well as raw metals. Birmingham, settled six years after the Civil War, is no repository of genteel southern tradition and/or moderation, has been keyed to violence, whether labor troubles in the 1930s or desegregation in the 1950s. And Birmingham's white country people, teeming in from piney woods to steel mills, view desegregation less as an abstract threat to be fended off by lawyers than as a specific, bread-and-butter threat to jobs, promotions, family security. Says Bull Connor: "If the North keeps trying to cram this thing down our throats, there's going to be bloodshed."

**Blast of Bombs.** This sort of prediction, oratorical in many areas of the South, has to be taken with seriousness in Vulcan's city. Reason: in the last decade, by minimal count of Birmingham's white newspapers, there have already been 22 dynamite bombings and four arson burnings attributable to race tensions. Fountain Heights and North Smithfield, where Negroes, with a go-ahead from federal courts, began moving in nine years ago to break the city's segregated housing patterns, are now known as "Dynamite Hill." The $18,000 home of the Negro woman who had won the lawsuit was torn by a dynamite blast days after the court decision. And many years, many blasts later, the ordeal turned to terror one night last July when three whites drove onto Dynamite Hill, tossed one bomb at a Negro home, lobbed another at the home of a white family that was talking about selling to Negroes. The police eventually got all three; one was convicted last week by a Jefferson County circuit court jury that recommended a 10-year prison sentence, with probation; the other two are out on bail awaiting trial.

Birmingham's best-known Negro leader, the Rev. Fred L. Shuttlesworth, a tough, thick-skinned, egocentric sort, has had his home bombed, his church bombed. Arrests in the case to date: nil. So Shuttlesworth has taken his protection into his own hands, now musters a guard of a dozen or so Negro volunteers at his church and home every night on shifts dusk to dawn.

**Silence of Fear.** In this situation, Birmingham's moderates mostly prefer to keep their thoughts to themselves. Result: a vacuum of leadership. Those businessmen who profess moderation run the risk, if not of dynamite, of economic reprisals such as loss of jobs, promotions, trouble with city licenses, city contracts, harassment on petty automobile offenses, tightening up on loans, etc. Mayor James Morgan, popular with businessmen, in office since 1937, is privately telling friends that he intends to resign next year — "I used to enjoy going to the City Hall. I don't anymore." Housewives who profess moderation run the risk of social ostracism. White ministers, asked to help improve communications between the races, reply only with generalities. Says one moderate: "It isn't enough that you are in favor of segregation. You've got to say so out loud or you're suspected of being on the other side."

Such segregationist groups as the Ku Klux Klan and White Citizens' Councils concentrate unerringly on keeping the moderates silent and leaderless. Method No. 1: Informers. One of the six men arrested in a Negro castration case turned out to be a Ku Klux Klan captain of intelligence—and a member of Alabama's interracial Council on Human Relations who had sat quietly through all council meetings. Method No. 2: Quick Mobilization. The Citizens' Councils have a chain-telephone-call system that can blanket the city in 12 hours. Method No. 3: Phone Threats. A Presbyterian minister who wrote to *The Birmingham News* last September simply to protest Orval Faubus' indictment of Presbyterian ministers as "brainwashed leftwingers" (*TIME*, Sept. 29) still gets regular, threatening, dead-of-night phone calls. And the thing that makes such psychological warfare real is the threat of dynamite. One Methodist minister, active in the hard-harassed Council on Human Relations, has moved his daughters, aged 3 and 1, into the back bedroom because of "fear of bombings."

This is why, in the death of leadership, the silence of fear, the bomb blasts of hatred, Birmingham, Vulcan's crucible, is the toughest city in the South, and likely to get tougher. It is also why the voice of a police chief, Bull Connor, has emerged as the voice of one of the great cities of the U.S.

*If the North keeps trying to cram this thing down our throats, there's going to be bloodshed.* — Bull Connor, quoted in *TIME,* December 15, 1958.

# "As Birmingham goes, so will go your future and the future of your children and your grandchildren."

Anne Braden, a white Civil Rights activist in Louisville, Kentucky, who often helped ACMHR get national press, penned this promotional piece to describe segregated conditions in Birmingham. She details ACMHR's track record challenging those conditions and the opposition it met. Widely distributed, the piece gets the Birmingham Movement story out to a large national audience.

## Excerpts: "They Challenge Segregation At Its Core," Anne Braden, ACMHR Promotional Piece, 1959.

Not only are the schools, the parks, the buses segregated in the traditional Southern pattern, in Birmingham, it is unlawful for Negroes and White people to play checkers together, to play baseball together, to eat in the same places or attend the same educational or entertainment events, unless they are completely separated. Housing has become rigidly segregated; the better jobs, in public agencies as well as private industry, are denied to Negroes. . . .

All these regulations and prohibitions are rigidly enforced by an inflexible police department and by terror. People have been arrested for simply meeting in a private home to discuss these injustices. . . .

Mr. Shuttlesworth described the movement in a recent statement as part of the "world wide revolution which is a divine struggle for the exaltation of the human race." He added:

*We here in Birmingham, Ala., are part of this universal fight between Right and Wrong. . . . To this cause we are dedicated without reservation and there can be no turning back. . . .*

In Birmingham, Negroes are today carrying on their struggle for equality virtually alone. Repeatedly, they have asked officials to sit down and discuss their grievances in a give-and-take manner. This was done on every issue before court action was taken as a last resort. The answer has always been silence.

Wherever you live, if you believe in human dignity and brotherhood, Birmingham Negroes are fighting your battle. Birmingham is the strongest bastion in America. When equality and right win there, the key line of segregationist defense will be breached. From then on, victory for human rights will be easier everywhere. As Birmingham goes, so will go your future and the future of your children and your grandchildren.

*Birmingham in a sense is the test for America's future.*

## Excerpts: President's Annual Report to the ACMHR, June 5, 1959.

Our goal today is the same as three years ago — First Class Citizenship for all Americans without regard for race, creed or color. We affirm our pledge of June 5, 1956, to 'press forward, persistently for freedom and Democracy, and the removal from our society any forms of 2nd Class Citizenship.' This means on buses, in school, in recreational facilities, in housing areas, in job opportunities, and any other public utilities. We are not dismayed that our Birmingham City Hall displays Shut Eyes, Closed Minds, and a Hostile Attitude toward any Civil Rights for Negroes. Neither do our hearts quake at the openly declared hostility to Negroes by the Governor of our state, nor the sudden rise in outright Klannish activity in the past few months. We only pray that our methods will always be Christian, that no hate will ever be found nor practiced in our hearts and actions, and that out of the intensity of this struggle we Negroes will become more religious, more consecrated, better Americans.

*This photograph of a slum ghetto appears in* People in Motion, *a summary of the Movement, also prepared by Anne Braden and the Southern Conference Educational Fund, Inc, (SCEF), John Spragens, Jr., SCEF, 1965.*

# ACMHR Under Arrest. Legal Cases & Lawyers

Although court challenges were not dramatic, ACMHR pursued them, racking up an impressive number of cases and appeals. These challenges helped serve as a lawful basis for civil rights reform, when no one else, most notably Birmingham's public officials, took positive action to end segregation. Legal appeals also advanced opportunities for Birmingham's black lawyers, especially attorneys Arthur Shores, Orzell Billingsley, Jr., and Oscar Adams, Jr.

*If the Ku Klux Klan doesn't stop you, the police can; and if the police fail, then the courts will.* — Rev. Shuttlesworth, *Ebony*, 1971.

Attorney Arthur Shores, Robert Adams, The Birmingham News.

*Negroes generally were swearing by him (Shuttlesworth); white people, generally were swearing about him. But wherever he was being cussed or discussed, there seemed from both groups a grudging admiration for the man.* — Francis Mitchell, "A Controversial Minister," 1960.

---

DO **NOT DESTROY THIS RECORD.**

5726 1/5

POLICE DEPARTMENT
BUREAU OF IDENTIFICATION
BIRMINGHAM, ALABAMA

DATE: October 16 1963

RECORD OF ARRESTS AND CRIMINAL HISTORY OF: Fred Lee Shuttlesworth

COLOR: Negro    SEX: Male    BUREAU NUMBER: 94206    FBI NUMBER 2 958 033

| CITY | NAME AND NUMBER | DATE | CHARGE | DISPOSITION |
|---|---|---|---|---|
| Sheriff Office Birmingham,Ala. | Fred Shuttlesworth #15850 | 8-4-40 | Distilling | 2-14-41 placed on 2 yrs probatio: |
| Sheriff Office Birmingham,Ala. | Fred Shuttlesworth #15850 | 8-29-42 | Probation Violation | No record of a Disposition at Courthouse |
| PD Birmingham Ala. | Fred Shuttlesworth | 2-7-58 | Reckless Driving | 3/3/58 $25-$5 Cost: |
| PD Birmingham Ala | Fred Shuttlesworth | 1-8-60 | Speeding | 1-15-60 $10-$5 Cos' |
| PD Birmingham Ala | Fred Lee Shuttlesworth | 3-31-60 | Vagrancy Warr | 4-1-60 Vag. Warr released. 4-4-60 aiding & abetting violation of City Ord. $105-180 days Appealed. 10.11/60 Case Dismissed. |
| PD Birmingham Ala | Fred Lee Shuttlesworth | 4-2-60 | Vagrancy Aiding & Abetting Violation of City Ord. | 4-3-60 Vag. Rel. 4-4-60 Aid. & Abet Viol. City Ord. $105-180 days. Appealed. Appeal affirmed and appea to Ala. Supreme Court 5-30-61. |
| PD Birmingham Ala. | Fred Lee Shuttlesworth | 5-17-61 | Failure to obey Officer; Interf. with officer. | 5-17-61 $105-180 d ref. to obey;$105-180 days interf wi officer; $10 & 24 hrs for contempt. Appealed intf with officer; found |

*David L. Boozer*
Superintendent of Police Recor

*Rev. Shuttlesworth's Record of Arrests and Criminal History Page 1 of 5, Police Department, Bureau of Identification, Bureau Number: 94206, October 16, 1963, Birmingham Public Library Archives Police Surveillance Files.*

Rev. Shuttlesworth's Civil Rights-era Birmingham criminal record includes 19 arrests on 35 counts including charges for Reckless Driving, Speeding, Vagrancy, Failure to Obey Lawful Command of An Officer, Disorderly Conduct, Conspiring to Commit a Breach of Peace, Unlawful Assembly, Parading Without a Permit and Interfering With an Officer in Discharge of Duty.

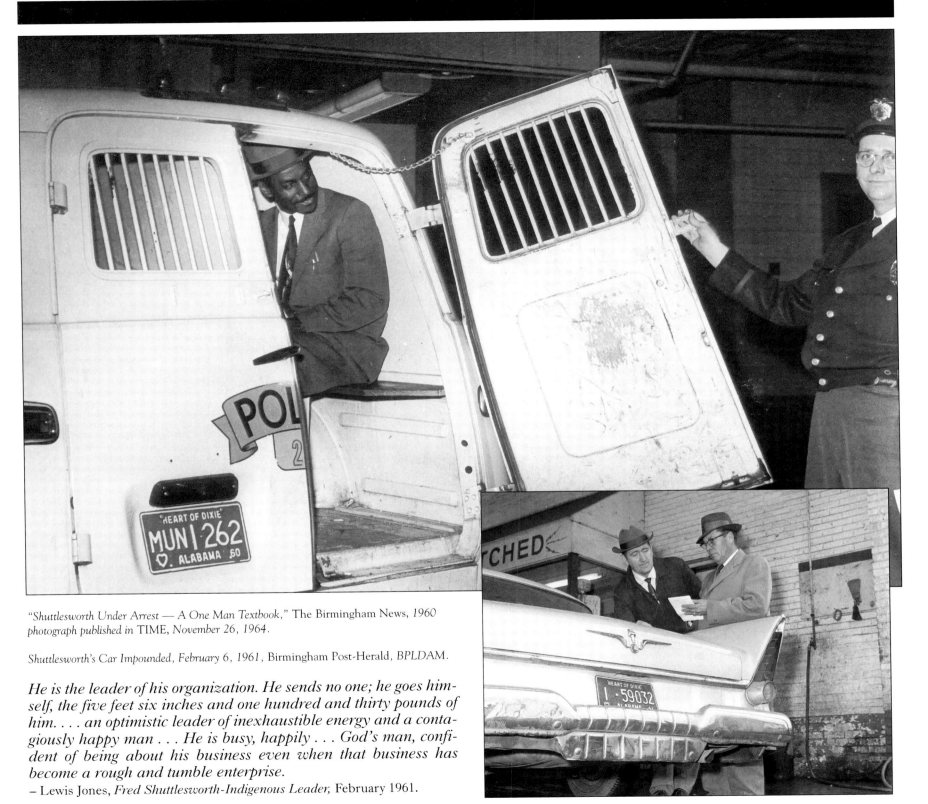

"*Shuttlesworth Under Arrest — A One Man Textbook,*" The Birmingham News, 1960 photograph published in TIME, November 26, 1964.

*Shuttlesworth's Car Impounded, February 6, 1961, Birmingham Post-Herald, BPLDAM.*

*He is the leader of his organization. He sends no one; he goes himself, the five feet six inches and one hundred and thirty pounds of him. . . . an optimistic leader of inexhaustible energy and a contagiously happy man . . . He is busy, happily . . . God's man, confident of being about his business even when that business has become a rough and tumble enterprise.*
– Lewis Jones, *Fred Shuttlesworth-Indigenous Leader,* February 1961.

# "FEAR AND HATRED GRIP BIRMINGHAM
## Racial Tension Smoldering After Belated Sitdowns"

Reprinted from *The New York Times*, by Harrison E. Salisbury, April 12, 1960, Pages 1 & 28.

In 1960, students across the South began to sit in at lunch counters and to combat segregation in public accommodations. While a Nashville group was most successful, the Birmingham group organized by Miles College student Frank Dukes with assistance from Rev. Shuttlesworth and ACMHR also achieved significant success, both in imposing economic hardship on the merchants and in broadening the base of support for the Movement in the larger Birmingham community. Students, who had neither jobs nor mortgages to lose, would play an increasing role in Movement activities across America.

Birmingham press did not cover these sit-ins. Pulitzer Prize-winning journalist Harrison Salisbury chronicles sit-in action and reprisals to the sit-ins in his front-page story, the first major national story describing the Birmingham situation:

**BIRMINGHAM, Ala., April 8** — From Red Mountain, where a cast-iron Vulcan looks down 500 feet to the sprawling city, Birmingham seems veiled in the poisonous fumes of distant battles.

On a fine April day, however, it is only the haze of acid fog belched from the stacks of the Tennessee Coal and Iron Company's Fairfield and Ensley works that lies over the city.

But more than a few citizens, both white and Negro, harbor growing fear that the hour will strike when the smoke of civil strife will mingle with that of the hearths and forges.

It is not accidental that the Negro sit-in movement protesting lunch-counter segregation has only lightly touched brooding Birmingham. But even those light touches have sent convulsive tremors through the delicately balanced power structure of the community.

The reaction has been new manifestations of fear, force and terror punctuated by striking acts of courage.

No New Yorker can readily measure the climate of Birmingham today.

## Tension Is High in Birmingham

Police Commissioner Eugene Connor was elected in 1958 on race hate platform.

Rev. F. L. Shuttlesworth has been arrested twice; his church and home bombed.

Whites and blacks still walk the same streets. But the streets, the water supply and the sewer system are about the only public facilities they share. Ball parks and taxicabs are segregated. So are libraries. A book featuring black rabbits and white rabbits was banned. A drive is on to forbid "Negro music" on "white" radio stations.

Every channel of communication, every medium of mutual interest, every reasoned approach, every inch of middle ground has been fragmented by the emotional dynamite of racism, reinforced by the whip, the razor, the gun, the bomb, the torch, the club, the knife, the mob, the police and many branches of the state's apparatus.

In Birmingham, neither blacks nor whites talk freely. A pastor carefully closes the door before he speaks. A Negro keeps an eye on the sidewalk outside his house. A lawyer talks in the language of conspiracy.

Telephones are tapped, or there is fear of tapping. Mail has been intercepted and opened. Sometimes it does not reach its destination. The eavesdropper, the informer, the spy have become a fact of life.

Volunteer watchmen stand guard 24 hours a day over some Negro churches. Jewish synagogues have floodlights for the night and caretakers. Dynamite attempts have been made against the two principal Jewish temples in the last 18 months. In 11 years, there have been 22 reported bombings of Negro churches and homes. A number were never reported officially.

### Community of Fear

Birmingham's whites and blacks share a community of fear. Some Negroes have nicknamed Birmingham the Johannesburg of America.

"The difference between Johannesburg and Birmingham," said a Negro who came South recently, from the Middle West, "is that, here, they have not yet opened fire with the tanks and big guns."

"I have lived in Alabama all my life," said a newspaperman. "Birmingham is going to blow one of these days. And, when that happens, that's one story I don't want to be around to cover."

"Remember," a businessman said, "Birmingham is no place for irresponsible reporting. Be careful of what you say and who you mention. Lives are at stake."

"I'm ashamed to have to talk to you off the record," said an educator. "It is not for myself. But these are not ordinary times. The dangers are very real and people up North must realize that."

"Excuse me," an educated Negro woman said. "But I just don't understand the white people around here. They seem to act so crazy. It doesn't make any sense. Don't they know there is a limit to what people will stand?"

"If you sow hate, you reap hate," said a Negro pastor.

### Quiet in Early Phases

When the Negro student sit-in movement

reached Birmingham 10 days ago it set in motion a sequence of events almost reflexive in character.

Birmingham had been quiet during the early phases of the student protests. Two months ago, a dozen Negro students went to a public park and began a brief "prayer for freedom." It was curtailed when the police arrested the students on a charge of public disorder.

Then on Thursday, April 2, ten Negro students went two by two into five downtown Birmingham stores. They made small purchases and sat at the lunch counters. All were arrested immediately on charges of trespassing. They were held 18 hours before being able to make bond.

The next 72 hours were busy ones for the Birmingham Police. They arrested three Negro ministers; the Rev. F. L. Shuttlesworth, the Rev. Charles Billups and the Rev. C. Herbert Oliver. Mr. Shuttlesworth was arrested twice on successive days.

The police also arrested Thomas Reeves, a 21-year-old white student at Birmingham-Southern College and part-time preacher, and Jessie Walker, a Negro student from Daniel Payne University.

Each of those arrested was charged with "vagrancy." In addition, Mr. Reeves and Mr. Oliver, who was hauled barefooted and in his bathrobe from his home, were charged with "intimidating a witness."

By Birmingham custom, persons charged with vagrancy are not admitted to bail. They are held incommunicado for three days. In actual practice, such a prisoner is sometimes permitted to make one telephone call. But not always. A person arrested on a vagrancy warrant simply disappears for three days. His friends and family may not know what has happened to him.

## A Favorite Technique

This is a favorite technique of Birmingham's Police Commissioner, Eugene Connor. Mr. Connor is a former sports broadcaster known as Bull because of the timbre of his voice. He served as Birmingham Police Commissioner for 16 years in the late 1930s and 1940s. His administration was a stormy one.

He went into eclipse for several years but made a comeback in 1958, running on a platform of race hate.

"Bull is the law in Birmingham, like it or not," a businessman said.

Mr. Connor is the author of many widely quoted aphorisms. He once said: "Damn the law—down here, we make our own law."

On another occasion, he declared: "White and Negro are not to segregate together."

"Only legitimate hold-ups will be investigated," he announced after evidence had been uncovered that some Birmingham robberies were inside jobs.

Mr. Shuttlesworth has been a frequent target of Mr. Connor's men. He has three cases on appeal. His church has been bombed twice. In one bombing, his home was destroyed. Both he and his wife were injured and a white pastor was badly manhandled by a Birmingham mob when the three of them sought to use the white waiting room of the local bus depot.

A test of the forces symbolized by Mr. Connor is now in the making—a product of the seismic Birmingham reaction to the Negro student sit-ins.

It centers on young Reeves. He is a slight youngster weighing about 137 pounds and standing five feet eight inches. He wears horn-rimmed glasses, suffers from asthma and is noticeably shy and diffident.

## Centers on Student

He has been charged by the police with "intimidating a witness." The witness presumably was one of the 10 Negro students arrested for sit-ins.

The parents of young Reeves have received threats of death. The youth has been restricted to the campus of Birmingham-Southern, technically on administrative probation. Actually, the step is for his physical protection.

A cross was burned on the Birmingham-Southern campus, possibly because of the Reeves case, possibly because 97 Birmingham-Southern students had signed a petition to Gov. John Patterson protesting his action in forcing Alabama College to expel Negro sit-in demonstrators. The petition did not protest segregation. It protested political interference with the academic process.

Dr. Henry King Stanford, president of Birmingham-Southern, has been subjected to extraordinary pressures. But he has not buckled under. He supported the right of his students to send their petition to Governor Patterson on the ground of academic freedom. When he was confronted with threats and demands that young Reeves be expelled, he again stood his ground. He declined to pre-judge the case.

## The Price of Courage

In Birmingham, this kind of courage does not come cheaply. Dr. Stanford has been told that the college's position in the Reeves case will cost it a minimum of $1,500,000. This is the amount that the college had hoped to raise in a drive for badly needed building funds this year.

But as one Birmingham citizen said, "You weigh the situation. You take the counsels of caution. You listen to the voices which say don't rock the boat. But, finally, the time comes when a man has to stand up and be counted."

If fear and terror are common in the streets of Birmingham, the atmosphere in Bessemer, the adjacent steel suburb, is even worse.

On the night the Birmingham police arrested Mr. Shuttlesworth, a band of floggers went to work in Bessemer.

One of the students who participated in the "prayer for freedom" lived in Bessemer. An evening or two later, seven carloads of hooded men roared into the street where the youngster lives with his mother and sister.

Armed with iron pipes, clubs and leather blackjacks into which razor blades were sunk, the men attacked the boy and his mother and sister. The mother and sister protected the boy with their bodies. The men broke a leg of the mother, smashed open her scalp and crushed her hands.

Forty-five minutes after the alarm had been given, the police arrived, but the band had fled. The next day two deputies visited the mother in the hospital. She recoiled in horror. They were two of those who had beaten her, she said. No charges were lodged.

"She is afraid to say anything," a man familiar with the case declared.

The list of beatings, intimidations and violence could be continued almost indefinitely. . . .

# The Freedom Ride Riot

The Congress for Racial Equality (CORE) organized the Freedom Rides, the rides on buses from the North to the South to protest segregation of interstate transportation facilities. The CORE group rode as far as Alabama where they were firebombed in Anniston and beaten by mobs in Birmingham and Montgomery. After the violence in Montgomery, the state of Alabama provided armed protection for the rides.

Rev. Shuttlesworth and ACMHR members helped make the Freedom Rides a success. Shuttlesworth coordinated the rides across Alabama, and personally rescued and nursed brutalized riders and assisted new riders to travel on. For his participation, Rev. Shuttlesworth was condemned by a front-page editorial in *The Birmingham News*, May 18, 1961.

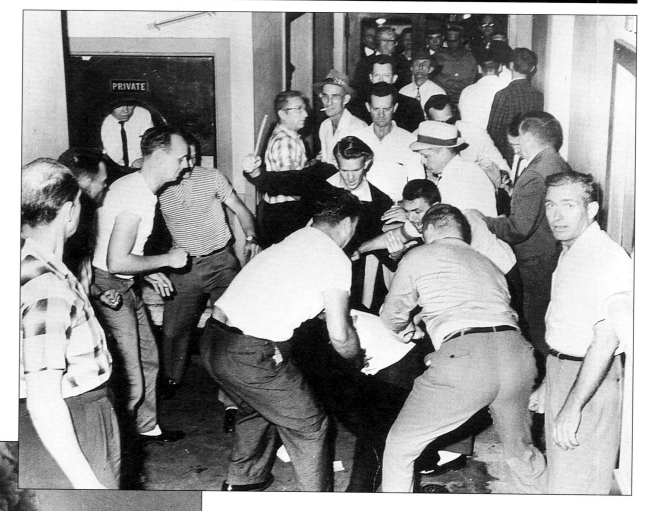

*This Greyhound bus, left, carrying an integrated group of Freedom Riders burns outside Anniston, Alabama. Klansmen slashed tires, gave chase and firebombed the vehicle. Rev. Shuttlesworth and ACMHR members rescued the riders. Another bus continued to Birmingham arriving on Mother's Day. The Birmingham News, May 15, 1961.*

*"SCENE AT STATION HERE (above)– This picture taken was at the Trailways Bus Station here yesterday of James A. Peck of New York just after he left the Atlanta-Birmingham bus. Peck is the man in dark trousers sinking to the floor under blows in foreground. The man whose rear protrudes to the right is Gary Thomas Rowe, Jr., the Klansman who turned FBI informant." Tommy Langston, Trailways Bus Station, Birmingham Post-Herald, Monday, May 15, 1961. This photograph is also published in newspapers around the world.*

**But fear and hatred did stalk Birmingham's streets yesterday.**
– *The Birmingham News*, front-page editorial, May 15, 1961.

*Freedom Rider James Peck with Wounds Bandaged. He survived a clubbing with an iron pipe. The Birmingham News. It takes 250 stitches to close Peck's head.*

*Of the Sunday terror, Commissioner of Public Safety 'Bull' Connor said – his police were not able to act because it was Mother's Day and many of them were off duty. His Excellency, the Governor of Alabama, John Patterson, said, 'I cannot accept the responsibility for a group of renegades who are here for the avowed purposes of stirring up trouble.'* – Howard K. Smith, CBS *Who Speaks for Birmingham?*, 1961.

# "Where Were the Police?"

Editorial Reprinted from the
*Birmingham Post-Herald,* May 15, 1961, Page 12.

Prompt arrest and prosecution of the gang of hoodlums who took the law in their own hands yesterday afternoon at the Trailways Bus Terminal is extremely important.

Failure of the police to preserve order and to prevent the outbreak of violence is deeply disturbing.

They must have had advance notice that trouble was likely and if so they should have had enough uniformed officers on the scene to make certain that order would be maintained and the public protected.

The so-called "Freedom Riders" came looking for trouble and they should have been handled just as all other law violators are handled. But they should have been protected against assault by a gang of thugs who also should have been jailed promptly.

That's what the people expect from their law enforcement agencies and that is what they will demand.

This incident in Birmingham and the one along the highway just outside Anniston are not to be dismissed lightly.

If we are to have an orderly society we must see that the law and regularly constituted authority are respected.

To let gangs get away with what happened here yesterday not only will undermine respect for the law but will invite more serious trouble.

That must not happen.

## *Political Reform*

*Sid N. Smyer, Sr., President, Chamber of Commerce and of Birmingham Realty Company, the real estate firm that founded Birmingham in 1871, and still owns substantial real estate in the Birmingham city center, Birmingham Public Library Archives.*

The Freedom Ride riot helped shift white elite opinion against Bull Connor. Downtown realtor Sidney Smyer, headed a group of leaders that began the process of changing Birmingham's form of government.

## *Who Speaks For Birmingham?* Airs

CBS producer David Lowe attended a mass meeting on March 13, 1961, at St. James Baptist Church and attempted to interview participants, requesting them to "tell their own story in their own words." Refusing to answer Lowe's questions, approximately 20 gave, instead, emotional testimonials describing arrests and mistreatment by the Birmingham police and the miserable conditions of living in a segregated city.

Produced over a nine-month period and narrated by CBS News Chief Washington correspondent Howard K. Smith, *Who Speaks for Birmingham?* reported "on the background and mood of Birmingham by letting some of the people of that community speak of and for their city." The 60-minute special aired over national television on May 18, just following the Freedom Ride riots.

## *"Go Forward - Not Knowing, But Trusting"*

**Rev. Shuttlesworth's Annual Address, June 5, 1961.**

We are really breaking the back of segregation when all of the hell and fury of the police force the city houses and the state houses are being turned loose upon the Negro leaders. In addition to already being involved in 14 civil or criminal cases, I have been arrested four times within the past two weeks, and have five criminal charges against me. So you see, it's neither an easy thing nor a play thing to lead in the cause of freedom.

But Jesus is my Director and my Captain; and woe unto me if I preach not the gospel — the social gospel of freedom and of peace and justice and humanitarianism. It is mine to suffer these indignities as a common criminal — arrested by the police and persecuted by the courts. But He knoweth the way I take, and when He hath tried me I shall come forth as gold. Weeping may endure for a night, but joy cometh in the morning. And victory will be ours.

# Dixie's Most Fearless Freedom Fighter Shuttlesworth is Leaving Ala.!

Excerpts: *The Courier*, by Trezzvant W. Anderson, June 10, 1961.

*The Courier* is a black weekly newspaper published in Pittsburgh and with a New York City edition.

**BIRMINGHAM, Ala.** — Alabama's greatest and most fearless "Freedom Fighter" — the Rev. Fred L. Shuttlesworth, 39, born and reared in Alabama — is going to leave Alabama, as of August 1st to accept the pastorate of a large Baptist Church in Cincinnati, Ohio.

Oldest of nine children, born in Mt. Meigs, Montgomery County, Ala., on March 18, 1922, Rev. Shuttlesworth has given his whole heart and soul to the cause of advancement of his people.

In 1956, when the Alabama courts banned the NAACP from acting in Alabama, it was Rev. Fred Shuttlesworth who rushed into the breach.

He called a statewide mass meeting in June, 1956, after the NAACP banning in May, 1956. At this mass meeting, the Alabama Christian Movement for Human Rights was born with Fred Shuttlesworth as president.

It bridged the gap between the people and the NAACP and the spark of freedom was kept alive.

Rev. Shuttlesworth has become the most abused and arrested Negro minister in modern history. His going to Cincinnati will not cause him to relinquish the reins of the ACMHR.

Large churches in three Midwestern cities had put in a bid for the services of the intrepid young minister who had laid his life on the line for his people in Alabama time and again.

Cincinnati, St. Louis and another large city sought him, but he finally decided upon Cincinnati, a city from which he can commute by air to his beloved Birmingham and continue the fight for first class citizenship for his followers.

It is quite obvious that whites in Birmingham will hail his leaving as a victory for their cause, but the cold realism of the situation is that, with a wife and three children to provide for, Rev. Mr. Shuttlesworth was rapidly becoming unable to do this on the salary of the small 500-member Bethel Church he has pastored since 1953 when he came here from Selma. . . .

It was in 1958 that Rev. Mr. Shuttlesworth became a national columnist for *The Courier* and his weekly column is an eagerly awaited gem each week by thousands of *Courier* readers.

His modesty keeps him from revealing his own record of personal sacrifices.

But these include: the Christmas 1956 bombing of his home in which the house was flattened to the ground. In August 1955, he led a delegation of five ministers to City Hall, presenting a petition from 77 ministers requesting Negro policemen.

In September 1955, he presented a petition signed by 4,500 Negroes and 119 whites asking for Negro policemen. He was main speaker at the NAACP Emancipation Rally in January 1956, and followed this up with organization of the ACMHR in June 1956 when the NAACP was outlawed in May 1956.

Since then, he and his organization have been the standard-bearers in the fight for freedom in Alabama. He has been brutally beaten by mobs which also stabbed and cut his faithful wife; has been jailed and arrested more times than can be counted.

His church has been bombed several times, and he has organized local bus rides to break down transportation segregation on Birmingham buses at the risk of his own life. He has a large number of suits against segregation now pending in Federal courts in Birmingham, and will return to the city to see that they are prosecuted to a final determination.

## Concluding Service and Friendship Hour at Bethel

This service marked the termination of Rev. Shuttlesworth's pastorate at Bethel Baptist Church. Rev. Shuttlesworth, who has accepted the pastorate of a much larger Cincinnati church, explained his decision which tripled his salary, as necessary to finance the education of his children (all of whom ultimately obtained masters degrees and one a doctorate and currently teach in high schools and college). Neither Bethel, nor Shuttlesworth, left the Movement.

## Legal and Civil Victories

By February of 1961, Rev. Shuttlesworth is a plantiff in 14 lawsuits involving civil rights. He is served four more injunctions during the Freedom Rides.

By the end of 1961, ACMHR had won several legal victories including its lawsuits challenging segregation on Birmingham buses, in the Terminal (railroad) station, in the City parks, as well as the playing of any games together, a city ordinance Rev. Shuttlesworth describes as "the backbone of segregation in the city."

*Yes, sir. I'm in 14 lawsuits about segregation now . . . . But I remember what Mama told me: 'Never set a hen on one egg; it just wastes the hen's time.'* – Rev. Shuttlesworth to Lewis Jones, February 1961.

## Pleas for Reason

*"Business Leaders Plea With City Commissioners,"* December 1961, Birmingham Post-Herald Collection, Birmingham Public Library Department of Archives and Manuscripts.

On October 24, 1961, U. S. District Court Judge H. H. Grooms had declared Birmingham's segregation of public parks illegal. This photograph shows Mayor Art Hanes listening to elite businessmen petitioning the city commission to desegregate rather than close Birmingham's 67 public parks. Mayor Hanes rebukes the businessmen for supporting desegregation in the city proper when they reside in the suburbs and refuse to be annexed into Birmingham. The commission closes the parks effective January 1, 1962.

# Birmingham Parks Closed

*"Solitary Negro stares at deserted Highland Park, closed along with other recreational areas to avoid desegregating them." Lynn Pelham, Saturday Evening Post, March 2, 1963, page 13. The city parks remain closed for three years.*

**JANUARY 25-MARCH 2, 1962**

# Shuttlesworth and Phifer Jailed

Having lost a Supreme Court case due to a technicality, ACMHR leaders Reverends Shuttlesworth and Phifer serve jail sentences (of 90 and 60 days, respectively) for attempts to desegregate the Birmingham buses. The jailings prompt a local and national outcry and build solidarity and funding for the Movement. While serving sentences, Shuttlesworth reported to the *Birmingham World* that he was working 12-hour days, seven days a week. Petitions addressed from the jail included one to City Hall to desegregate the jail.

*White people could grieve easier if I could be blamed with all the trouble between races.* – Rev. Shuttlesworth, ACMHR Mass Meeting, January 15, 1962.

*He is in jail but he has transformed it from a place of shame to a place of dignity. . .* – Rev. J. L. Ware, ACMHR Mass Meeting, February 12, 1962.

*Since Shuttlesworth and Phifer are in jail for just riding a bus, and the men that set fire and completely burned a bus are free, I am of great concern.* – Rev. Ed Gardner, ACMHR Mass Meeting, Ensley Baptist Church, February 19, 1962.

# Lincoln's Birthday Rally

ACMHR brought the Rev. Martin Luther King, Jr., to town to rally support for freeing Reverends Shuttlesworth and Phifer and spoke to a capacity crowd gathered at Sixteenth Street Baptist Church. He told the crowd that he had recently told President and Mrs. John Kennedy of plans to rid America of segregation.

*We are prepared to 'Walk In,' 'Sit In,' 'Ride in' or anything else that it takes to do away with segregation.* – Rev. Martin Luther King, Jr., ACMHR Mass Meeting, Sixteenth Street Baptist Church, February 12, 1962.

**MARCH-JUNE, 1962**

# "Boycott in Birmingham, Ala. . . ."
Excerpts from *Newsweek*, May 14, 1963, Page 28.

Students from Miles College, Daniel Payne College, Booker T. Washington Business College joined by white students from Birmingham-Southern College, led a "Selective Buying Campaign" against white merchants. They aimed to desegregate lunch counters, restrooms and drinking fountains, and to obtain jobs for Blacks as clerks and sales assistants.

"Spearheaded by student leader Frank Dukes at Miles College, a Negro institution, the boycott has as its object the hiring of Negro clerks and salesmen and the desegregation of lunch counters and rest-rooms in the stores. Estimating the city's 200,000 Negroes spend as much as $4 million a week (merchants say that figure is too high), the students have circulated pamphlets inquiring: 'Why spend four million dollars in Birmingham where you may be arrested for standing in one spot too long while in the company of your friends?' According to Dr. Lucius H. Pitts, 47, Miles College president, the boycott has been a 'beautiful' way to register protest. 'If Negroes had gone down and picketed they would have been beaten up and arrested,' Pitts said. 'I think Negroes recognized this so they set out to take the trigger mechanism out of the bomb.'

**APRIL 3, 1962**

### City Cuts Appropriations to Surplus Food Program

# Easter. Wear Your Overalls to Church

*Newberry's Popular Values for Easter*, Ads, The Birmingham News, March 28, 1962.

The Selective Buying Campaign boycott of downtown stores intensifies during the Easter shopping season, as large numbers of Blacks respond sympathetically to the students. "Wear Your Overalls to Church" catches on throughout the black community and is highly effective in limiting clothing sales. Many could contribute support to the Movement in this manner without fear of reprisal.

*If you were poor and you were black . . . you were going to lose your job if you demonstrated. With large and extended families, you had mouths to feed.* — Marion Perdue explaining why many Birmingham Blacks could participate within the safety of their churches, but not in public demonstrations.

## MAY 1962

## Shuttlesworth Invites King to Birmingham

At the Southern Christian Leadership Conference Meeting in Chattanooga, Rev. Shuttlesworth extends an invitation to the Rev. Martin Luther King, Jr., and the SCLC to come to Birmingham.

## JUNE 5, 1962

## A Call for Reason, Sanity and Righteous Perseverance in a Critical Hour

Rev. Shuttlesworth, Annual Message to the ACMHR, A. O. H. Church of God, June 5, 1962.

Our battle is hard but the end is not yet. There is yet much more land to be conquered. The forces of evil and darkness have already caused us untold misery and suffering; but we are ready to suffer even more that freedom might reign. For if freedom is worth living in, it is worth dying for. Already, the unjust officials and courts have caused us to spend over $72,000 in six years for bonds, court costs, transcripts, lawyer fees, etc. — and we are in debt even now thousands of dollars with several more cases which have to be filed. . . .

A final thought: But for the trials, tribulations, and successes of the Movement, there would be no Progress in Birmingham. The Selective Buying Campaign came about as a result of the parks decision and the jailing of Rev. Phifer and myself. It is led by the students and should be supported by every single Negro in this city and country. Let us support the efforts of our race to be free and stay out of town until the madness downtown gives way to sanity and reason. "Lift up your heads, Oh ye gates. Be ye lift up ye everlasting doors; and The King of Glory shall come in." He is our rock and our shelter; He is all we need and He will give us the victory. Amen.

## Voters Scrap City Commission

Voters oust the city commission form of government and approve a mayor-council system of public officials, effectively voting Bull Connor out of office. They wanted change. Mayoral elections are set for March 5, 1963. Shuttlesworth calls off a planned Selective Buying Campaign for Christmas. Joint ACMHR and SCLC demonstrations are set for April 2, 1963.

## 1962 Movement Meeting Churches

### as Recorded by the Birmingham Police

The 18 large and centrally located structures pictured on the following pages hosted 45 mass meetings recorded by the Birmingham Police during 1962. The number of meetings listed indicates the number of police reports remaining at Birmingham Public Library Archives. Meetings were averaging from 500 to 600 persons during 1962.

ACMHR, not pleased with police attending meetings, files suit against the police. At the trial in 1962, leading adversaries: Rev. Shuttlesworth, serving as ACMHR's lawyer, and staunch segregationist Police Commissioner Connor, face each other. Although ACMHR loses the case, Shuttlesworth makes the most of the opportunity.

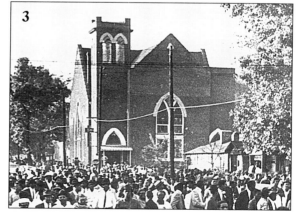

**\* 1. New Pilgrim Baptist Church,** Southside,
   9 recorded mass meetings

**2. First Baptist Church, Ensley,**
   6 recorded mass meetings

**3. St. James Baptist Church,** Northside,
   5 recorded mass meetings

**4. St. John A.M.E. Church,** Northside,
   3 recorded mass meetings

**\* 5. First Baptist Church, Kingston,**
   2 recorded mass meetings

**6. New Hope Baptist Church,** Avondale,
   2 recorded mass meetings

**7. Seventeenth Street A.O.H. Church,** Northside,
   2 recorded mass meetings

**\* 8. Sixteenth Street Baptist Church,** 1530 Sixth
   Ave. N., Northside, 2 meetings, used 1962-1963

**9. Tabernacle Baptist Church,** Northside,
   2 recorded mass meetings

10. **Zion Star Baptist Church,** Southside,
2 recorded mass meetings

11. **First Metropolitan Baptist Church,** Southside,
1 recorded mass meeting

12. **Macedonia Seventeenth Street Baptist Church,**
Northside, 1 recorded mass meeting

✱ 13. **Metropolitan A M.E. Zion Church,**
1530 Fourth Ave. N., Northside, 1 recorded
mass meeting, first used in 1961

✱ 14. **Peace Baptist Church,** Northside, 1 meeting

15. **Regular Missionary Baptist Church,**
East Birmingham, 1 recorded mass meeting

✱ 16. **St. Luke A. M.E. Church,**
North Birmingham, 1 recorded mass meeting

✱ 17. **Sardis Baptist Church,** Enon Ridge,
1 recorded mass meeting

18. **Thirgood C.M.E. Church,** 1 recorded mass
meeting first used in 1962.

# Bethel Baptist Church Bombed Again

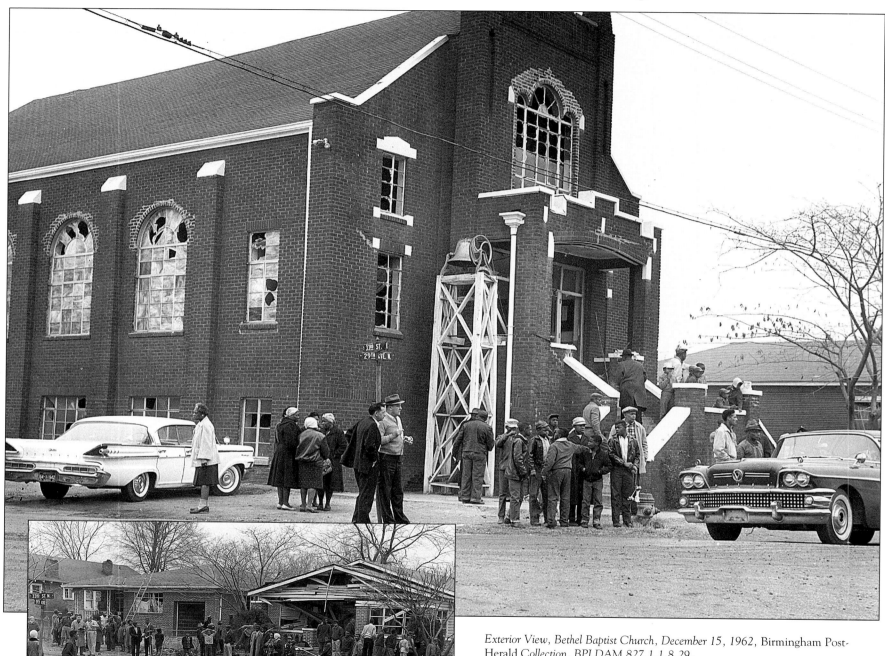

*Exterior View, Bethel Baptist Church, December 15, 1962, Birmingham Post-Herald Collection, BPLDAM 827.1.1.8.29.*

*Bomb Damage, Bethel Parsonage and James Revis House, December 15, 1962, 29th Avenue North, across from the Bethel Church, Birmingham Post-Herald Collection, BPLDAM 827.1.1.8.23.*

# BIRMINGHAM'S CIVIL RIGHTS CHURCHES

Monday Movement Meeting, June 23, 1958, East Thomas Baptist Church, Rev. J. A. Hayes, Pastor, ACMHR Souvenir Booklet, 1958.

*The Organization met every Monday night in different churches all over the city. The mass meetings were full of religious fervor and were so well attended by the faithful, 300 to 400 of whom attended regularly each Monday.* – Rev. Fred Shuttlesworth, 1998.

1.a **Abyssinia Baptist Church**
*1501 Ave. I, Ensley*

2.a **Bethel A.M.E. Church**
*1524 Ave. D, Ensley*
*ACMHR Treasurer W. E. Shortridge*

3.a,c **Bethel Baptist Church**
*3191 29th Ave. N., Collegeville,*
*ACMHR Headquarters, Rev. Fred Lee*
*Shuttlesworth, Pastor 1953-1961,*
*Rev. Vincent Provitt, 1961-1974*

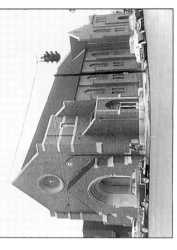

10.a **First Baptist Church of Kingston**
*4600 9th Ave. N., Kingston*

11. **First Baptist Church of Woodlawn**
*301 62nd St. S., Woodlawn*

12.a **First Ebenezer Baptist Church**
*420 Graymont Ave. W., Smithfield*
*Birmingham Historical Society*

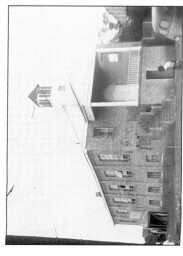

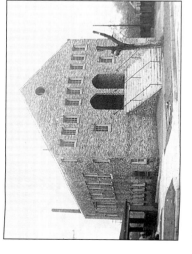

19. **Lily Grove Baptist Church**
*1015 3rd St. N., Druid Hills*

20. **Macedonia 17th Street Baptist Church**
*922 17th St. N., Northside*

21.a **Metropolitan A.M.E. Zion Church**
*1530 4th Ave. N., Northside*
*Rev. G. W. McMurray*

"Bomb damage at Bethel Baptist Church is viewed by Rev. V. C. Provitt, Blast occurred last December," Saturday Evening Post, March 2, 1963, page 15.

*This was a retaliatory bombing. The Klan showing the war was still on.*
— Rev. Shuttlesworth, 1998.

James Revis House with Guard Room at right of porch, 3236 29th Ave. N., December 15, 1962, Birmingham Post-Herald Collection, BPLDAM 827.1.1.8.28. Bethel member and Movement supporter James Revis built the guard house to provide protection for Rev. Shuttlesworth and the church.

# "Segregation Now! . . . Segregation Forever!"

During the 1960s, Alabama Governor George Corley Wallace represented the implacably segregationist South. His inaugural address expresses the new governor's segregationist stance, a stance he would personally put into action later in the year when he physically barred the attempt of two Blacks and Federal marshals to enroll students at the University of Alabama.

### Excerpts From George Wallace's Inaugural Address:

THIS NATION WAS NEVER MEANT to be a unit of one, but a unit of many, and so it was meant in our racial lives. Each race, within its own framework, has freedom to teach, to instruct, to develop, to ask for and receive deserved help from others of separate racial station; but if we amalgamate into the one unit as advocated by the Communist philosopher, then the enrichment of our lives, the freedom for our development is gone forever. We become, therefore, a mongrel unit of one under a single all-powerful government. And we stand for everything, and for nothing. . . .

Today, I have stood where Jefferson Davis stood, and took an oath to my people. It is very appropriate then that from this Cradle of the Confederacy, this very heart of the great Anglo-Saxon Southland, that today we sound the drum for freedom as have our generation of forebears before us time and again down through history. Let us rise to the call of freedom-loving blood that is in us and send our answer to the tyranny that clanks its chains upon the South. In the name of the greatest people that ever trod this earth, I draw the line in the dust and toss the gauntlet before the feet of tyranny. . . . And I say: segregation now . . . segregation tomorrow . . . segregation forever.

Let us send this message back to Washington . . . that from this day we are standing up, and the heel of tyranny does not fit the neck of the upright man . . . that we intend to take the offensive and carry our fight for freedom across this nation, wielding the balance of power we know we possess in the Southland . . . that we, not the insipid bloc voters of some section . . . will determine in the next election who shall sit in the White House . . . that from this day . . . from this hour . . . from this minute . . . we give the word of a race honor that we will tolerate their boot in our face no longer . . . and let those certain judges put that in their opium pipes of power and smoke it for what it is worth.

What I have said about segregation goes double this day . . . and what I have said to you about some Federal judges goes triple this day.

Not so long ago men stood in marvel and awe at the cities, the buildings, the schools, the autobahns that the government of Hitler's Germany had built, just as centuries before they stood in wonder at Rome's building . . . but it could not stand, for the system that built it rotted the foundations of what God meant that men should be.

George Wallace at the Alabama Statehouse, Inauguration Day Parade, January 14, 1963, Robert Adams, The Birmingham News.

*We become, therefore, a mongrel unit of one under a single all-powerful government . . . . and we stand for everything and for nothing.* – George Wallace, January 14, 1963.

Today that same system on an international scale is sweeping the world. It is the "changing world" of which we are told . . . it is called new and "liberal." . . .

It is as old as the oldest dictator. It is degenerate and decadent. As the national racism of Hitler's Germany persecuted a national minority to the whim of a national majority . . . so the international racism of the liberals seeks to persecute the international white minority to the whim of the international colored majority . . . so that we are footballed about according to the favor of the Afro-Asian bloc. . . .

Let us, as Alabamians, grasp the hand of destiny and walk out of the shadow of fear . . . and fill our divine destination.

I shall "stand up for Alabama" as governor of your state . . . you stand with me . . . and we, together . . . can give courageous leadership to millions of people throughout this nation who look to the South for their hope in this fight to win and preserve our freedoms and liberties. . . .

# Movement Meeting Churches April-May 1963

During April and May 1963, police recorded 45 meetings held at 15 churches. The police were not present at many mass meetings nor at secret strategy committee meetings held daily during the spring campaign at First Congregational Church on "Dynamite Hill" in Smithfield.

## Top Meeting Churches 1961-1963

### As reported by the Birmingham Police.

During these years, 15 churches served as meeting churches. With the success of the legal tests and the Freedom Rides, attendance increased so that larger churches were selected to accommodate the numbers of ACMHR members who attended Movement Meetings.

**St. James Baptist Church,**
22 recorded mass meetings

**New Pilgrim Baptist Church,**
17 recorded mass meetings

**First Baptist Church of Ensley,**
11 recorded mass meetings

**New Hope Baptist Church,**
10 recorded mass meetings

**Sixteenth Street Baptist Church,**
10 recorded mass meetings

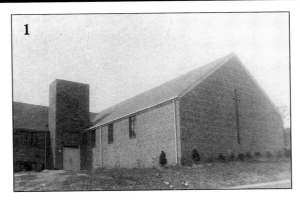

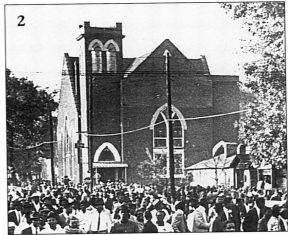

* 1. **First Congregational Church,** 1022 Center St. N., Smithfield, secret stategy committee meetings held daily from April 2 to May 10, 1963
2. **St. James Baptist Church,** Northside, 12 recorded mass meetings
* 3. **Sixteenth Street Baptist Church,** Northside, 7 recorded mass meetings

4. **Sixth Avenue Baptist Church,** Southside, 1529 Sixth Avenue South, first used in April of 1963, 7 recorded mass meetings & a funeral
* 5. **New Pilgrim Baptist Church,** Southside, 4 recorded mass meetings
6. **First Baptist Church of Ensley,** Ensley, 5 recorded mass meetings

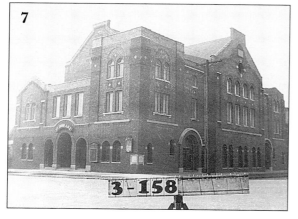

7. **St. John A.M.E. Church,** Northside, 2 recorded mass meetings & the Robertson funeral
* 8. **St. Luke A.M.E. Church,** North Birmingham, 2 recorded mass meetings
9. **St. Paul A.M.E. Church,** Smithfield, 2 recorded mass meetings

* 10. **St. Paul (United) Methodist Church,** Northside
11. **Metropolitan A.M.E. Zion Church,** Northside, 1 recorded mass meeting
12. **Seventeenth Street A.O.H. Church of God,** Northside, 1 recorded mass meeting

13. **Tabernacle Baptist Church,** Northside, 1 recorded mass meeting
14. **Thirgood C.M.E. Church,** Northside, 1 recorded mass meeting
† 15. **Thirty-Second Street Baptist Church,** Southside, 1 recorded mass meeting

## *Mass Meetings begin the Birmingham Campaign*

*Crowds gathered along Sixth Avenue outside St. James Baptist Church, The Birmingham News Collection BPLDAM 1076.7.95.*

St. James Baptist Church, located five blocks west of Kelly Ingram Park in a densely populated residential district, performed stalwart duty for the Movement. St James often hosted mass meetings. The 93-year old Rev. Marzett L. Thornton, St. James's pastor from 1922 to 1964, supports Rev. Shuttlesworth and his "young fellows" because "he wanted to live to see Freedom come." Three back-to-back nightly meetings at St. James open the Birmingham campaign of April 1963. St. James hosted more recorded meetings than any other church during the period 1961 to 1963.

### Albert Boutwell wins Mayoral election.

*I have been advised that a small group of racial agitators under familiar leadership have undertaken to embarrass both the present and the incoming city governments by sit-in demonstrations. . . . The so-called leaders of these sit-in demonstrations, indifferent to the welfare of either people of the city, have seized this chance to create strife and discord.* – Birmingham Mayor-elect Albert Boutwell, "Prepared Comments," *The Birmingham News,* April 3, 1963. Birmingham voters vote Connor out of office, but he refuses to leave.

# "Birmingham Manifesto"

## The Patience of an Oppressed People Can Not Endure Forever

### Reprinted from the *Birmingham World*, April 6, 1963, page 2.

Rev. Shuttlesworth, Rev. N. H. Smith, Jr., and Rev. Wyatt T. Walker drafted and circulated the "Birmingham Manifesto" the day before demonstrations began. The statement details the litany of evils that had precipitated the nonviolent demonstrations.

"The patience of an oppressed people cannot endure forever. The Negro citizens of Birmingham for the last several years have hoped in vain for some evidence of good faith, resolution of our just grievances.

"Birmingham is a part of the United States and we are bona fide citizens. Yet the history of Birmingham reveals that very little of the democratic process touches the life of the Negro in Birmingham. We have been segregated racially, exploited economically, and dominated politically. Under the leadership of the Alabama Christian Movement for Human Rights, we sought relief by petition for the repeal of city ordinances requiring segregation and the institution of a merit hiring policy in city employment. We were rebuffed. We then turned to the system of the courts. We weathered set-back after set-back, with all of its costliness, finally winning the terminal, bus, parks and airport cases. The bus decision has been implemented begrudgingly and the parks decision prompted the closing of all municipally-owned recreational facilities with the exception of the zoo and Legion Field. The airport case has been a slightly better experience with the exception of hotel accommodations and the subtle discrimination that continues in the limousine service.

"We have always been a peaceful people, bearing our oppression with super human effort. Yet we have been the victims of repeated violence, not only that inflicted by the hoodlum element but also that inflicted by the blatant misuse of police power. Our memories are seared with painful mob experience of Mother's Day 1961 during the Freedom Ride. For years, while our homes and churches were being bombed, we heard nothing but the ranting and ravings of racist city officials.

"The Negro protest for equality and justice has been a voice crying in the wilderness. Most of Birmingham has remained silent, probably out of fear. In the meanwhile, our city has acquired the dubious reputation of being the worst big city in race relations in the United States. Last fall, for a flickering moment, it appeared that sincere community leaders from religion, business and industry discerned the inevitable confrontation in race relations approaching. Their concern for the city's image and commonwealth of all its citizens did not run deep enough. Solemn promises were made, pending a postponement of direct action, that we would be joined in a suit seeing the relief of segregation ordinances. Some merchants agreed to desegregate their rest-rooms as a good faith start, some actually complying, only to retreat shortly thereafter. We hold in our hands now broken faith and broken promises.

"We believe in the American Dream of democracy, in the Jefferson doctrine that "all men are created equal and are endowed by their Creator with certain unalienable rights, among these being life liberty and the pursuit of happiness."

"Twice since September we have deferred our direct action thrust in order that a change in the city government would not be made in the hysteria of a community crisis. We act today in full concert with our Hebraic-Christian tradition the law of morality and the Constitution of our nation. The absence of justice and progress in Birmingham demands that we make a moral witness to give our community a chance to survive. We demonstrate our faith that we believe that the beloved community can come to Birmingham.

"We appeal to the citizenry of Birmingham, Negro and white, to join us in this witness for decency, morality, self-respect and human dignity. Your individual and corporate support can hasten the day of "liberty and justice for all." This is Birmingham's moment of truth in which every citizen can play his part in her larger destiny.

## Project C (Confrontation) A joint campaign of ACMHR & SCLC

*The purpose of the campaign was to make Bull Connor the target, to fill the Birmingham jails, to override segregation, and be treated equally before the law.*
– Rev. Shuttlesworth, 1998.

*Bull Connor, Street View, Robert Adams,* The Birmingham News.

*The mystery of the whole situation is how can these simple home folks be talked into going to jail by a bunch of rabble-rousers.* – Bull Connor, quoted in, *The Alabama Christian Movement for Human Rights and the Birmingham Struggle for Civil Rights,* Glenn Eskew, 1989.

# The Non-Violence Ethic

## ACMHR Pledge

I HEREBY PLEDGE MYSELF, MY PERSON AND BODY, TO THE NONVIOLENT MOVEMENT. THEREFORE, I WILL KEEP THE FOLLOWING TEN COMMANDMENTS:

1. MEDITATE daily on the teachings and life of Jesus.
2. REMEMBER always that the nonviolent movement in Birmingham seeks justice and reconciliation – not victory.
3. WALK and TALK in the manner of love, for God is love.
4. PRAY daily to be used by God in order that all men might be free.
5. SACRIFICE personal wishes in order that all men might be free.
6. OBSERVE with both friend and foe the ordinary rules of courtesy.
7. SEEK to perform regular service for others and for the world.
8. REFRAIN from the violence of fist, tongue, or heart.
9. STRIVE to be in good spiritual and bodily health.
10. FOLLOW the directions of the movement and the captain on a demonstration.

I sign this pledge, having seriously considered what I do and with the determination and will to persevere.

Name _____

Besides demonstrations, I could also help the Movement by: (Circle the proper items)  Run errands, Drive my car, Fix food for volunteers, Clerical work, Make phone calls, Answer phones, Mimeograph, Type, Print signs, Distribute leaflets.

Alabama Christian Movement for Human Rights
Birmingham Affiliate of S. C. L. C.  • F. L. Shuttlesworth, President

*Movement demonstrators signed the pledge card above, agreeing to act nonviolently. The 1963 photograph shows marchers praying while waiting to be arrested and loaded into paddy wagons for transport to the city jail. The Birmingham News, 1963.*

# "B" (Birmingham) Day
# Opening Day of the Campaign

*First Sit-In, Woolworth's Lunch Counter Sit-In, April 3, 1963, Birmingham Post-Herald Collection BPLDAM 827.1.1.6.11.*

## Sit-Ins At Retail Stores

Project C began with an economic boycott of downtown retail stores. Small groups of demonstrators seek to be served a meal at these establishments. Rev. Abraham Woods, Jr., and his brother, Rev. Calvin Woods, lead the sit-in to the lunch counters of the leading retail stores — Woolworth's, Loveman's, Pizitz, Kress and Britt's — all located along 19th Street. Managers close the counters for the day. Pictured above on the right are Rev. Calvin Woods, 29, and George Harris, 71, who sit at the Woolworth's counter from about 10:15 a.m. until 2:00 p.m. Later in the afternoon, they and 18 others are arrested at Britt's Department Store.

*We can turn Birmingham upside down and right side up by non-violence.* – Rev. Martin Luther King, Jr., Mass Meeting, St. Luke A.M.E. Church, April 29, 1963.

*You can rest assured that I will fill the jail full of any persons violating the law as long as I'm in City Hall.* – Ex-commissioner Connor, at the April 4 trials of the first sit-in demonstrators.

# First March of the Campaign to City Hall

*Marchers With Arms and Voices Joined While Singing "We Shall Overcome," Courtyard, A. G. Gaston Motel, Fifth Avenue at 16th Street, Robert Adams, The Birmingham News. SCLC leaders, middle row: Rev. Wyatt T. Walker, Rev. Shuttlesworth, Rev. King, Dorothy Cotton, Bernard Lee and Rev. Ralph Abernathy.*

Rev. Shuttlesworth leads the first march of the Birmingham Campaign to City Hall to pray and petition newly elected Mayor Albert Boutwell for legal rights. Marchers gather at the Gaston Motel, a site closer to City Hall than Thirgood C.M.E. Church, 1027 Seventh Avenue, the planned starting point. Here, they sing for 15 minutes before heading out. Police set up a blockade.

*We are embarking on a mission to break down the barrier of segregation in Birmingham. Hard segregation is entrenched in Birmingham. We in Atlanta have come to the aid of Fred Shuttlesworth. He called on us and we were glad to come because of the injustice in Birmingham.* – Rev. Martin Luther King, Jr., ACMHR Mass Meeting at St. James Baptist Church, April 5, 1963, on the eve of the first march pictured above.

*March Leader, Rev. Shuttlesworth (left, with back turned), assembling the men and women marchers two by two, while Rev. Martin Luther King, Jr., (right) and other SCLC leaders see them off, Courtyard, A. G. Gaston Motel, April 6, 1963, Birmingham Police Department Surveillance Collection BPLDAM 1125.11.20.A-2.*

The previous evening at the Mass Meeting, Rev. Shuttlesworth announced that "he wanted to drink some of that white water in the City Hall and see if it tasted any better than the colored water." Marchers intend to pray at City Hall in protest of parade permits denied.

*March Leaders Rev. Fred Shuttlesworth (not visible) behind Police Capt. George Wall and Rev. Charles Billups With Praying Marchers, U. S. Post Office (today's Vance Courthouse), April 6, 1963, Fifth Avenue North between 18th and 19th Streets, The Birmingham News Collection.*

*When they stopped the march, we knelt to pray and were arrested.*
– Rev. Shuttlesworth, 1998.

## March on City Hall

Marchers gather at St. Paul Methodist Church, 1500-Sixth Avenue North, six blocks from City Hall. More than 1,000 persons line the avenue. Police set up a road block two blocks away at 17th Street and convey to the march leaders that persons crossing 17th Street will be arrested. When the marchers cross the intersection, police stop them. The group kneels for a brief prayer and is arrested for "parading without a permit."

*Capt. G. V. Evans halts march leaders: Rev. N. H. Smith, Jr., Rev. A. D. Williams King and Rev. John Thomas Porter, The Birmingham News, April 8, 1963, page 2.*

*The first few days of the campaign went peacefully. But we knew it was in the nature of Bull to be a bull. Bull thought he was going to try (Albany Police Chief Laurie) Pritchett's strategy, but his own philosophy wouldn't allow him to do that. He couldn't just let us march. That was what we wanted to do.*
– Rev. Shuttlesworth, 1998.

### APRIL 10, 1963

### State Court Injunction Against Protests, Demonstrations, Boycotts, Sit-ins and Marches

Circuit Court Judge William Jenkins issues an injunction against demonstrations.

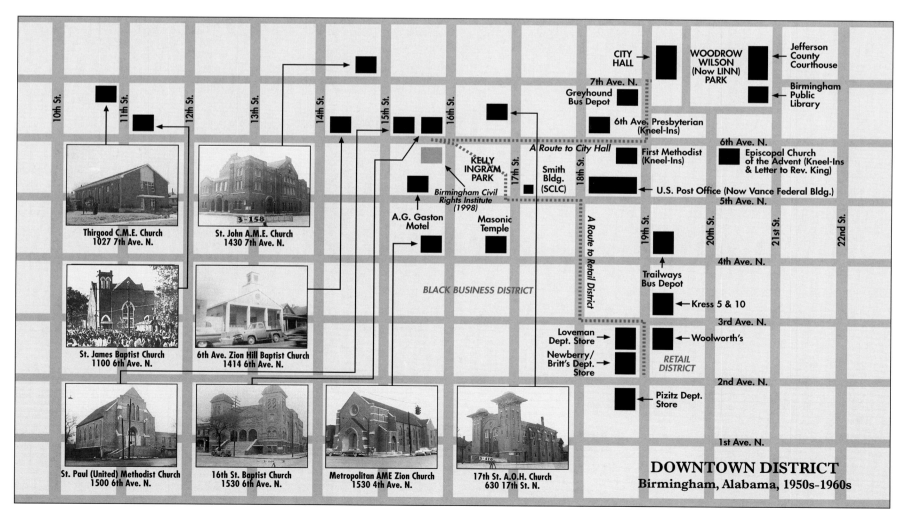

CITY HALL

WOODROW WILSON (Now LINN) PARK

Jefferson County Courthouse

7th Ave. N.
Greyhound Bus Depot

Birmingham Public Library

6th Ave. Presbyterian (Kneel-Ins)

6th Ave. N.

*A Route to City Hall*

First Methodist (Kneel-Ins)

Episcopal Church of the Advent (Kneel-Ins & Letter to Rev. King)

KELLY INGRAM PARK

Smith Bldg. (SCLC)

U.S. Post Office (Now Vance Federal Bldg.)
5th Ave. N.

*Birmingham Civil Rights Institute (1998)*

A.G. Gaston Motel

Masonic Temple

*A Route to Retail District*

**BLACK BUSINESS DISTRICT**

Trailways Bus Depot

4th Ave. N.

Kress 5 & 10

3rd Ave. N.

Loveman Dept. Store

Woolworth's

Newberry/ Britt's Dept. Store

RETAIL DISTRICT

2nd Ave. N.

Pizitz Dept. Store

1st Ave. N.

Thirgood C.M.E. Church
1027 7th Ave. N.

St. John A.M.E. Church
1430 7th Ave. N.

St. James Baptist Church
1100 6th Ave. N.

6th Ave. Zion Hill Baptist Church
1414 6th Ave. N.

St. Paul (United) Methodist Church
1500 6th Ave. N.

16th St. Baptist Church
1530 6th Ave. N.

Metropolitan AME Zion Church
1530 4th Ave. N.

17th St. A.O.H. Church
630 17th St. N.

## DOWNTOWN DISTRICT
### Birmingham, Alabama, 1950s-1960s

# Good Friday March on City Hall

In a show of solidarity, the "Big Three" Movement leaders —the Reverends Shuttlesworth, Abernathy and King, left to right, in work shirts highlighting the boycott of white stores— emerge from the Gaston Motel to join marchers who waited at Sixth Avenue Zion Hill Baptist Church, 1414 Sixth Avenue, April 12, 1963, Birmingham Police Department Surveillance Files, BPLDAM1125.11.20 A-1.

Rev. Shuttlesworth, "not ready to be arrested, goes back to do a little more work" and is arrested later in the day. He puts up bond and is released quickly.

"Chanting marchers end in jail —The Rev. Ralph Abernathy, left, and the Rev. Martin Luther King, Jr., are shown (above) leading an attempted march on City Hall Friday. They were halted by police and the demonstrators jailed. The long line of marchers chanted integration verses as they moved along." AP/Wide World Photos, The Birmingham News, April 13, 1963, page 2.

Rev. King and Rev. Abernathy lead the singing demonstrators. Birmingham police break up the march and arrest some of the leaders and 50 marchers. Rev. King remains imprisoned for eight days. (The Birmingham Civil Rights Institute exhibits the solitary cell where King was confined.)

## Mass Meeting Vote for Civil Disobedience

Participants vote to continue the marches despite, and in violation of, the state court ruling prohibiting them.

## "White clergymen urge local Negroes to withdraw from demonstrations."

In this *Birmingham News* article published just beneath the photograph of the Good Friday march (facing page), eight leading white, Christian and Jewish clergymen denounce the protests, praise the Police Department's handling of the marches and ask that redress be sought through the courts. Honest, open negotiations between local black middle-class leaders and whites are suggested as a preferable way to settle racial issues:

"We rather agree with certain local Negro leadership (middle class leaders not associated with the Movement) which has called for honest and open negotiation of racial issues in our area.

And we believe this kind of facing of issues can best be accomplished by citizens of our own metropolitan area, white and Negro, meeting with their knowledge and experience of the local situation. All of us need to face that responsibility and find proper channels for its accomplishment. . . .

When rights are consistently denied, a cause should be pressed in the courts and negotiations among local leaders, and not in the streets."

### APRIL 14, 1963 • EASTER SUNDAY

## Kneel-ins

Small groups begin the first of four Sunday kneel-ins at Northside and neighborhood churches. Seven persons attend Easter services at the First Baptist and First Presbyterian churches downtown. Other worshipers are quietly turned away from three, white churches.

## March to the Jail

Streaming out of Thirgood C. M. E. Church, this march led by the Reverends A. D. King, Nelson Smith, Jr., and John Thomas Porter and Frank Dukes, the former Miles College student leader, begins with glorious singing as marchers head down 11th Street. Bull Connor and 50 police halt the marchers, and the more than 500 bystanders who follow them. When rocks are thrown at the police, the police use night sticks and billy clubs to break up the crowd.

*"Birmingham's New Nine-Member City Council Sworn Into Office,"* The Birmingham News, *April 15, 1963, page 1.*

Mayor-elect Boutwell is also sworn into office, but shares duties with Commissioner Connor who refuses to vacate his office.

## Send The Trouble-Makers Away!

Editorial Reprinted from the *Birmingham Post-Herald,* April 15, 1963, Page 10.

"If the Negroes responsible for the demonstrations which have shattered the tranquility of our community for more than a week are really interested in improving the lot of the Negro they will send the trouble-makers away and put an end to the lawlessness they have fostered. . . . "

The local press report statements and actions by the Rev. Martin Luther King, Jr., and other SCLC staff who appear to be the spokesmen and organizers of the campaign. Rev. Shuttlesworth and ACMHR leaders find little mention and are not directly involved in negotiations to end the demonstration or to achieve racial progress. Thus, the "outside agitator" theory spreads and King replaces Shuttlesworth not only as the scapegoat for racial ills, but also as the ultimate victor in the Birmingham struggle.

# Letter from the Birmingham Jail
## by Martin Luther King, Jr.

Reprinted from The American Friends Service Committee, Philadelphia, May 1963.

Rev. King, confined in a solitary cell at the Birmingham jail, receives the newspaper in which Birmingham's white clergy condemn the Birmingham demonstrations and call for talks with middle-class black and white leaders. King begins his reply writing on the margins of the newspaper, later his notes spill onto toilet tissue, paper scraps and finally to a legal pad supplied by visiting lawyers. Released to the press on April 18, the letter makes little first impression and is not well received by the white clergymen. The first published version of the letter includes these excerpts.

Birmingham City Jail
April 16, 1963

Bishop C. C. J. Carpenter
Bishop Joseph A. Durick
Rabbi Milton L. Grafman
Bishop Paul Hardin
Bishop Nolan B. Harmon
The Rev. George M. Murray
The Rev. Edward V. Ramage
The Rev. Earl Stallings

My dear Fellow Clergymen,

While confined here in the Birmingham City Jail, I came across your recent statement calling our present activities "unwise and untimely." Seldom, if ever, do I pause to answer criticism of my work and ideas. If I sought to answer all of the criticisms that cross my desk, my secretaries would be engaged in little else in the course of the day and I would have no time for constructive work. But since I feel that you are men of genuine goodwill and your criticisms are sincerely set forth, I would like to answer your statement in what I hope will be patient and reasonable terms.

I think I should give the reason for my being in Birmingham, since you have been influenced by the argument of "outsiders coming in." I have the honor of serving as president of the Southern Christian Leadership Conference, an organization operating in every Southern state with headquarters in Atlanta, Georgia. We have some eighty-five affiliate organizations all across the South—one being the Alabama Christian Movement for Human Rights. Whenever necessary and possible we share staff, educational, and financial resources with our affiliates. Several months ago our local affiliate here in Birmingham invited us to be on call to engage in a nonviolent direct action program if such were deemed necessary. We readily consented and when the hour came we lived up to our promises. So I am here, along with several members of my staff, because we were invited here. I am here because I have basic organizational ties here. Beyond this, I am in Birmingham because injustice is here. Just as the eighth century prophets left their little villages and carried their "thus saith the Lord" far beyond the boundaries of their home town, and just as the Apostle Paul left his little village Tarsus and carried the gospel of Jesus Christ to practically every hamlet and city of the Graeco-Roman world, I too am compelled to carry the gospel of freedom beyond my particular home town. Like Paul, I must constantly respond to the Macedonian call for aid.

Moreover, I am cognizant of the interrelatedness of all communities and states. I cannot sit idly by in Atlanta and not be concerned about what happens in Birmingham. Injustice anywhere is a threat to justice everywhere. We are caught in an inescapable network of mutuality tied in a single garment of destiny. Whatever affects one directly affects all indirectly. Never again can we afford to live with the narrow, provincial "outside agitator" idea. Anyone who lives inside the United States can never be considered an outsider anywhere in this country.

You deplore the demonstrations that are presently taking place in Birmingham. But I am sorry that your statement did not express a similar concern for the conditions that brought the demonstrations into being. I am sure that each of you would want to go beyond the superficial social analyst who looks merely at effects, and does not grapple with underlying causes. I would not hesitate to say that it is unfortunate that so-called demonstrations are taking place in Birmingham at this time, but I would say in more emphatic terms that it is even more unfortunate that the white power structure of this city left the Negro community with no other alternative.

In any nonviolent campaign there are four basic steps: (1) collection of the facts to determine whether injustices are alive; (2) negotiation; (3) self-purification; and (4) direct action. We have gone through all of these steps in Birmingham. There can be no gainsaying of the fact that racial injustice engulfs this community. Birmingham is probably the most thoroughly segregated city in the United States. Its ugly record of police brutality is known in every section of this country. Its unjust treatment of Negroes in the courts is a notorious reality. There have been more unsolved bombings of Negro homes and churches in Birmingham than any city in this nation. These are the hard, brutal, and unbelievable facts. On the basis of these conditions Negro leaders sought to negotiate with the city fathers. But the political leaders consistently refused to engage in good faith negotiation.

Then came the opportunity last September to talk with some of the leaders of the economic community. In these negotiating sessions certain promises were made by the merchants—such as the promise to remove the humiliating racial signs from the stores. On the basis of these promises Rev. Shuttlesworth and the leaders of the Alabama Christian Movement for Human Rights agreed to call a moratorium on any type of demonstrations. As the weeks and months unfolded we realized that we were the victims of a broken promise. The signs remained. As in so many experiences of the past we were confronted with blasted hopes, and the dark shadow of a deep disappointment settled upon us. So we had no alternative except that of preparing for direct action, whereby we would present our very bodies as a means of laying our case before the conscience of the local and national community. We were not unmindful of the difficulties involved. So we decided to go through a process of self-purification. We started having workshops on nonviolence and repeatedly asked ourselves the questions, "Are you able to accept blows without retaliating?" "Are you able to endure the ordeals of jail?"

We decided to set our direct action program around the Easter season, realizing that with the exception of Christmas, this was the largest shopping period of the year. Knowing that a strong economic withdrawal program would be the by-product of direct action, we felt that this was the best time to bring pressure on the merchants for the needed changes. Then it occurred to us that the March election was ahead, and so we speedily decided to postpone action until after election day. When we discovered that Mr. Connor was in the run-off, we decided again to postpone action so that the demonstrations could not be used to cloud the issues. At this time we agreed to begin our nonviolent witness the day after the run-off.

This reveals that we did not move irresponsibly into direct action. We too wanted to see Mr. Connor defeated; so we went through postponement after postponement to aid in this community need. After this we felt that direct action could be delayed no longer.

You may well ask, "Why direct action? Why sit-ins, marches, etc.? Isn't negotiation a better path?" You are exactly right in your call for negotiation. Indeed, this is the purpose of direct action. Nonviolent direct action seeks to create such a crisis and establish such creative tension that a community that has constantly refused to negotiate is forced to confront the issue. It seeks so to dramatize the issue that it can no longer be ignored. I just referred to the creation of tension as a part of the work of the nonviolent resister. This may sound rather shocking. But I must confess that I am not afraid of the word tension. I have earnestly worked and preached against violent tension, but there is a type of constructive nonviolent tension that is necessary for growth. Just as Socrates felt that it was necessary to create a tension in the mind so that individuals could rise from the bondage of myths and half-truths to the unfettered realm of creative analysis and objective appraisal, we must see the need of having nonviolent gadflies to create the kind of tension in society that will help men rise from the dark depths of prejudice and racism to the majestic heights of understanding and brotherhood. So the purpose of the direct action is to create a situation so crisis-packed that it will inevitably open the door to negotiation. We, therefore, concur with you in your call for negotiation. Too long has our beloved Southland been bogged down in the tragic attempt to live in monologue rather than dialogue.

One of the basic points in your statement is that our acts are untimely. Some have asked, "Why didn't you give the new administration time to act?" The only answer that I can give to this inquiry is that the new administration must be prodded about as much as the outgoing one before it acts. We will be sadly mistaken if we feel that the election of Mr. Boutwell will bring the millennium to Birmingham. While Mr. Boutwell is much more articulate and gentle than Mr. Connor, they are both segregationists dedicated to the task of maintaining the status quo. The hope I see in Mr. Boutwell is that he will be reasonable enough to see the futility of massive resistance to desegregation. But he will not see this without pressure from the devotees of civil rights. My friends, I must say to you that we have not made a single gain in civil rights without determined legal and nonviolent pressure. History is the long and tragic story of the fact that privileged groups seldom give up their privileges voluntarily. Individuals may see the moral light and voluntarily give up their unjust posture; but as Reinhold Niebuhr has reminded us, groups are more immoral than individuals.

We know through painful experience that freedom is never voluntarily given by the oppressor; it must be demanded by the oppressed. Frankly I have never yet engaged in a direct action movement that was "well timed," according to the timetable of those who have not suffered unduly from the disease of segregation. For years now I have heard the word "Wait!" It rings in the ear of every Negro with a piercing familiarity. This "wait" has almost always meant "never." It has been a tranquilizing thalidomide, relieving the emotional stress for a moment, only to give birth to an ill-formed infant of frustration. We must come to see with the distinguished jurist of yesterday that "justice too long delayed is justice denied." We have waited for more than three hundred and forty years for our constitutional and God-given rights. The nations of Asia and Africa are moving with jet-like speed toward the goal of political independence, and we still creep at horse and buggy pace toward the gaining of a cup of coffee at a lunch counter.

I guess it is easy for those who have never felt the stinging darts of segregation to say wait. But when you have seen vicious mobs lynch your mothers and fathers at will and drown your sisters and brothers at whim; when you have seen hate-filled policemen curse, kick, brutalize, and even kill your black brothers and sisters with impunity; when you see the vast majority of your twenty million Negro brothers smothering in an air-tight cage of poverty in the midst of an affluent society; when you suddenly find your tongue twisted and your speech stammering . . .

# Sixteenth Street Baptist Church Becomes the Departure Point

In the final phase of the Birmingham campaign, thousands participate in marches to City Hall and the retail district, the two focal points of the campaign's efforts. ACMHR-SCLC joint demands include four points to be achieved before demonstrations are called off: better employment opportunities, desegregation of downtown lunch counters, release of those imprisoned and creation of a biracial committee to work out plans for gradual desegregation of public accommodations.

Sixteenth Street Baptist Church, due to its large size and prominent location on Kelly Ingram Park, as well as its proximity to SCLC headquarters and to the A. G. Gaston Motel where Rev. King and SCLC staff stayed, both on Kelly Ingram Park, became the staging ground for the major mass demonstrations. Most news media covered the scene at this park and this church, giving the impression that the Movement "happened" here.

*On steps of Sixteenth Street Baptist Church, Movement Choir Director Carlton Reese (in the white shirt with arm raised, left) leads marchers in song. Across Sixth Avenue in Kelly Ingram Park, spectators, not Movement folks, cheer the marchers on to victory over segregation. Charles Moore, Black Star, photograph originally published in Life Magazine, May 17, 1963.*

# D Day • Children's Crusade Begins

*Children exiting Sixteenth Street Baptist Church, Robert Adams, The Birmingham News.*

Beginning May 2, children join the demonstrations. Initially, high school and college students are to demonstrate, but many arrive with their little brothers and sisters who insist in their right to join the fight for freedom. In groups of 20 to 50, they pour out of Sixteenth Street Baptist Church and other churches in the residential neighborhood at the same time. Organizers and older students coordinate movements with walkie-talkies.

Ten groups make it through police lines to City Hall. The children kneel to pray for city officials and sing freedom songs while police locate vehicles (including sheriff's cars and county school buses) to transport them to jail. Seven hundred persons are arrested and bond set at $500 per student.

*Our little folks made it to City Hall today to pray. Nobody else has been able to do it. . . . All we want to do is just walk, but everywhere we went the police blocked our way. They (the police) sure were tired."* – Rev. Shuttlesworth, Mass Meeting, Sixth Avenue Baptist Church, May 2, 1963.

*So let's all meet at the 16th Street Church Friday, Saturday and Sunday mornings and go from there to freedom.* – Rev. James Bevel who, with SCLC coordinator Wyatt Tee Walker and others, organized the Children's Marches, Mass Meeting, Sixth Avenue Baptist Church, May 2, 1963. Some 2,000 persons attended this mass meeting.

## Double-D Day

Groups of singing school children heading out from Sixteenth Street Baptist Church, just after noon, some heading across Kelly Ingram Park to the retail district, some to City Hall. May 3, 1963, UPI/Corbis-Bettmann 1378209.2.

*The doors of the church were flung open and the marchers poured forth chanting: "We're going to walk, walk, walk, Freedom. . . Freedom. . . Freedom.* – Birmingham Post-Herald, May 4, 1963, page 2.

*In a sense the freedom songs are the soul of the movement. . . . I have stood in a meeting with hundreds of youngsters and joined in while they sang, "Ain't Gonna Let Nobody Turn Me Round." It is not just a song; it is a resolve. A few minutes later, I have seen those same youngsters refuse to turn around before a pugnacious Bull Connor in command of men armed with powerful hoses. These songs bind us together, give us courage together, help us to march together.*– Rev. Martin Luther King, Jr., *Why We Can't Wait,* 1964.

On May 3, Reverends Shuttlesworth and King hold a joint press conference and indicate that demonstrations will continue until Movement objectives are met. Some 2,000 children arrive at Sixteenth Street Baptist Church for morning instruction sessions. Just after noon, several hundred students pour from the church and are arrested. As the jails are nearly full, Bull Connor decides to forcibly end the marches, rather than arrest the demonstrators.

As television cameras roll and reporters record, Bull Connor bellows: "Let 'em have it!" Bull lets 'em have it. To contain the marchers within the church, firemen turn on their hoses. Firemen also hose the crowds of 300 to 400 onlookers in the park. After 20 minutes of hosing, the police K-9 units arrive with their dogs. Onlookers throw rocks and bottles at law enforcement personnel. This evening, nightly news viewers across America watch in revulsion.

The Children's Crusade stuns Birmingham, galvanizes Blacks across the city and sends shock waves through America's collective conscience.

Firemen breaking up demonstrations, wide view from the 400 Block of 18th Street, looking South across town to Vulcan Park and the heavily forested Red Mountain. To close access to the retail district and contain demonstrations in "the Negro section," firemen had taken up positions such as this one. Robert Adams, The Birmingham News.

*Photographers Charles Moore with bystanders, policeman and dog, Kelly Ingram Park, The Birmingham News, May 3, 1963.*

Here bystanders, who appear daily in Kelly Ingram Park, purposely taunt a police dog to secure a good PR/media shot for Black Star photographer Charles Moore (center top). Birmingham police use dogs to control crowds and disperse demonstrators.

Fire hoses and police dogs provide lasting images of brutality in Birmingham. Best known images are those of Charles Moore. Trained as a U. S. Marine combat photographer, Moore shot for the *Montgomery Advertiser* in the 1950s before signing with Black Star. His famous photographs appear in *Life* Magazine's May 17, 1963 pictorial essay on the Birmingham demonstrations and later in *Powerful Days*, a collection of his Civil Rights photography.

## Mass Demonstrations Continue

*"5/4/1963-Birmingham, AL — During a mass rally of more than 3,000 Negroes protesting segregation, these three demonstrators hold hands for strength against the water. The force of these streams of water, used by riot police sent many demonstrators to the ground." UPI/Corbis Bettmann U1378208-29.*

On May 4, just after noon, children stream once again from Sixteenth Street Baptist Church and the A. O. H. Church of God. Firemen use stronger water from high pressure hoses that knock marchers off their feet from as far as 50 yards away. Two hoses are equipped with monitor guns, devices which permit use of two hoses with one spray. More than a thousand persons are jailed for participating in the marches.

U.S. Attorney General Robert Kennedy deplores the use of children in the marches. President John Kennedy states the sights of the assault in Birmingham make him sick, and that now he can "well understand why the Negroes of Birmingham are tired of being asked to be patient." The President dispatches two Assistant Attorneys, Burke Marshall and John Doar, to help mediate the dispute.

# *"Walk to Freedom"*

A scheduled Movement Meeting begins at 4:00 p.m. at New Pilgrim Baptist Church on Fifth Avenue South. Just after 7:00 p.m., and rather spontaneously, a decision is made for worshipers to walk to the city jail, a few blocks away to pray for the thousands confined there and in other makeshift facilities. Rev. Charles Billups leads the walk.

Fearing attempts will be made to enter the jail grounds, police and firemen stand guard with hoses and dogs for crowd control. The photograph, on the right, records a scene outside the Traffic Engineering Building where City officials halt the marchers.

*When Bull Connor ordered them to turn back, they knelt in prayer. Connor continued ranting until Rev. Billups dared him: "Turn on the water! Loose the dogs! We ain't going back. Forgive them, O Lord." As the marchers headed toward the firemen, the firemen aimed and nothing happened. Nearby hydrants remained pressure-less. Convinced of a miracle, singing and praying the worshipers walked on and conducted a prayer vigil under the watchful eye of the firemen.* – This account is summarized from William Witherspoon's *Martin Luther King, Jr. . . . To the Mountaintop.*

*Danella Jones Bryant, Gary Haynes, UPI staff photographer, UPI/Corbis-Bettmann U1378289-9. Photograph published in Life, May 17, 1963.*

*"Hoses Are Ready But Unused In Alabama — Fire hoses are trained on a group of 2,000 Negroes in Birmingham, Ala., as a march is organized on the jail where hundreds of demonstrators are being held. The march was peaceful and the hoses were not used. Only a few arrests were made in contrast to previous days when large numbers of anti-segregation demonstrators were pulled in. A prayer meeting was held in a park."* Al Kuettner for UPI; Quentin Perry, photographer, Scott Newspapers, Atlanta, Birmingham World, May 11, 1963, page 1.

*Participants, prayer service, Behrens (now Memorial) Park, Sixth Avenue South between 6th and 9th Streets, across from the Birmingham Jail, Charles Moore, Black Star.*

A prayer service in the small park lasts about 15 minutes. Participants sing, "Above My Head I Hear Freedom in the Air," and then return to the New Pilgrim Church.

*The demonstration Sunday was the closest thing to a victory the Negro community has won here in a month of racial strife which has resulted in nearly 1,500 arrests, many of them elementary school children.*– Al Kuettner, UPI, *Birmingham World,* May 11, 1963, page 1.

## Kneel-ins

Sunday's march followed kneel-ins at 21 Birmingham churches. Eight congregations receive and seat Movement members for services.

# Comedian Dick Gregory Leads March of 800 Children to City Hall

*Children Marching Two-By-Two from Sixteenth Street Baptist Church, May 6, 1963. UPI/Corbis Bettmann UI378400-6.*

By May 6, march organizers have the drill down pat. In the morning, more than 2,000 children arrive at Sixteenth Street to march for freedom. Just after noon, they march long enough to fill footage for the nightly television newscasts, often proceeding a single block to school buses waiting at the 17th Street to pick them up. In marching that one block, they filled sufficient footage to accomplish a media coup.

Rev. Martin Luther King, Jr., and a dapperly dressed Dick Gregory address the 2,000 school children assembled at the Sixteenth Street church. Police close off Kelly Ingram Park. They and firemen stand by to control the crowds. In rapid succession, marchers emerge from the church. Police arrested 800 demonstrators, many at 17th Street where they load them into county school buses.

By the close of the day, 2,300 adults and children overfill the city jail, the county jails in Birmingham and Bessemer, the 4-H Barracks at the Alabama State Fairgrounds and whereever else they can temporarily house the demonstrators. The next day, ACMHR leader Rev. Edward Gardner estimates bonds ($500-per-child) at well over $200,000. The county sheriff complains about the $300-per-day cost of feeding the inmates.

*We got them in there from 6, 9, 10 and 12 years old and they want freedom. . . . If they (the parents and grandparents) quit worrying so much and pray more, they would be better off. . . . We are not concerned about dogs and water. We are concerned about freedom.* – Rev. Edward Gardner, ACMHR, Vice President, Mass Meeting, May 7, 1963, Sixteenth Street Baptist Church.

*"Youth protestors in holding cell," Basement Room, Birmingham City Hall, May 6, 1963, Charles Moore, Black Star. The children wait for transport to makeshift jails.*

*We walked from Western-Olin High School to 16th Street. Going to jail was COOL! . . . Until we got hungry.* – Victor Blackledge

## Mass Meetings at Multiple Churches

Attendance is so large, the meetings are held at several churches at the same time. Host churches include St. John A.M.E., St. Paul Methodist, Thirgood CME, Sixteenth Street Baptist, New Pilgrim Baptist and Sixth Avenue Baptist.

**MAY 7, 1963**

## Marches Continue

*"After being forced to march around the block near the staging point, the Sixteenth Street Baptist Church, Negro demonstrators 5/7 made a successful break toward the downtown area with a mass exodus across Kelly Ingram Park."* Original UPI caption, The Birmingham News *photograph.*

On May 7, Movement officials decide to send the students, not straight into the police and fire barricades, but to span out in diverse directions and converge in the retail district at noon.

*"City-Owned Armored Vehicle Stands By During Demonstration. . . . Riot wagon was not used, however, as Negroes pour into downtown."* The Birmingham News, *May 7, 1963, page 3.*

## Retail District Swamped With Freedom Soldiers

*Students (left) race past a police blockade at 18th St. & Third Ave. N. headed for the retail district. This photograph looks south on 18th St. Robert Adams, The Birmingham News, May 7, 1963, page 2.*

*Massive demonstrations (above) in the retail district. View looking east along Third Ave. at 19th St. Robert Adams, The Birmingham News, May 7, 1963.*

According to *Birmingham Post-Herald* reports, "2,000 swarmed the retail district (other estimates place the figures at 3,000 persons). Police and fire vehicles jam the intersection. Traffic is halted for 30 minutes as noontime shoppers and demonstrators crowd the streets. Small groups of demonstrators enter stores and sing freedom songs. ACMHR stalwarts kneel and pray. After about an hour, the marchers return to Sixteenth Street Baptist Church. Meanwhile, several hundred demonstrators walk to City Hall to pray and also return to the church.

*View looking east along Third Ave. Demonstrators stand peaceably on the sidewalks. Robert Adams, The Birmingham News.*

*At Kelly Ingram Park, Rev. Fred Shuttlesworth (right) raises his hand to calm the crowd and end demonstrations that almost got out of hand here 5/7. Several persons were injured when a rock- and bottle-throwing incident erupted during the height of demonstrations." UPI/Corbis Bettmann U1378625-3.*

## Rev. Shuttlesworth Hospitalized

After checking to see that all the children are out of the immediate vicinity, Rev. Shuttlesworth heads into the church. Firemen "put some water on the Reverend." The spray slams him against a front door to the basement, injuring him and flooding the church, which the firemen then pump dry. Doctors find his blood pressure elevated and give him "hypos" to calm him down. Negotiations proceed without Shuttlesworth.

*"I wish I'd been there to see him carried away in a . . . hearse."*
– Bull Connor to a newspaper man, May 8, 1963.

*Bull Connor made the impact greater, but the dynamics would have taken effect without Bull Connor and the dogs. . . . When the demonstrations were so massive and the economic withdrawal program was so tight, literally, the town was paralyzed.*– Rev. Andrew Young, SCLC Assistant, "And Birmingham," 1971.

## *Temporary Moratorium*

State officials order 575 highway patrolmen into Birmingham. Armed with tear gas, sawed off shot guns and submachine guns, the troopers patrol every corner the next day.

With state troopers on every corner of the city center, federal negotiators together with Black moderates — Arthur Shores, John Drew, Lucious Pitts and Andrew Young — representing the Blacks and representatives of the white business community – Sid Smyer, David Vann, Roper Dial and Edward Norton — reach a settlement to end the demonstrations. The settlement accepts promises and establishes a committee of middle class citizens to achieve racial reform in Birmingham. President Kennedy and Rev. King plan a joint press conference to simultaneously announce the end of protest marches. ACMHR, co-sponsor with SCLC of the Birmingham campaign, is not represented at the negotiating table.

### MAY 8, 1963

### Feud at the Top

When Rev. Shuttlesworth learns of the moratorium achieved without consultation and without real solution to the issues, as had been the agreement when ACMHR and SCLC combined forces, he checks himself out of the hospital and explodes. Shuttlesworth demands concessions from the white business leaders. King announces a 24-hour pause in demonstrations. Within two days a settlement is reached.

*"JFK Discusses Situation Here. Kennedy 'gratified' at racial progress," Associated Press wirephoto, The Birmingham News, May 9, 1963, page 2, AP/Wide World Photoss.*

# An Accord With Conscience

Excerpts reprinted from Robert Gutwillig's, "Six Days in Alabama," *Mademoiselle,* now Conde Nast Publications, Inc., September 1963.

Decide to wait. Stand in sun scrunched together with photographers, newsreel cameras, sound equipment, reporters, and Negro spectators. On balcony of the A. G. Gaston Motel stand perhaps a hundred Negroes, leaning on railing. Spirits high.

King, Shuttlesworth, Abernathy show at 2:30. Ministers sit down at round white metal table with hole in middle for umbrella pole. No umbrella. Table full of microphones and wires. Ministers introduced by Wyatt Tee Walker, another minister, one of King's assistants. Tall, thin, light-skinned. Very Ivy League. Walker says Shuttlesworth just out of hospital. Shuttlesworth knocked over by hose Tuesday, taken to hospital in ambulance, prompting Bull Connor's locally famous remark about wishing he had "gone in hearse." He will read statement first and go back to hospital.

Shuttlesworth: "The City of Birmingham has reached an accord with its conscience." Reads statement about four points of agreement: desegregation of lunch counters, rest rooms, drinking fountains in stages over ninety days; better job opportunities; release (on bond) from jail of demonstrators; further communications between whites and Negroes within two weeks.

Burst of applause and cheering. Shuttlesworth dark, almost gaunt, man. Two gold teeth flashing. Reads statement slowly and softly. Had heard he was real firebrand. Seems exhausted.

King reads long statement. Looks just like pictures. Very professional. Statement very mild and moderate. Also oleaginous. Keeps referring to Birmingham unironically as "The Magic City," as it is called on signs by Chamber of Commerce. Everything King says about restraint and avoidance of violence in wake of "victory for democracy and the whole citizenry of Birmingham - Negro and white" very reasonable. But he reads statement like a politician. Is

politician. What else could he be by now? Negroes applauding, cheering.

Reporters fire questions. King answers most of them. Says: ". . . greatest and most significant victory for justice in deep South. . . Never has a community offered so much so quickly . . . [Negro negotiators] dealing with large community of merchants, business, industrial, and community leaders, not with either city government. . . Negotiated with economic power structure, and political power structure must follow through."

Shuttlesworth fields a few questions about whether he believes white negotiators are sincere and will implement agreements. He is known to have pressed for more specific agreements than King and hasn't gotten them. Suddenly stands up, saying he isn't feeling well. Applause as he leaves. Collapses in crowd behind me. King keeps on talking. Doesn't notice, or thinks he should go on anyway. Shuttlesworth taken away.

Reporters keep pressing King about generality of settlement. Feeling seems to be that whites negotiated out of fear of economic collapse (Negroes have been boycotting downtown stores for weeks) and impending violence; Negroes compromised because of pressure from U.S. Government (King speaks warmly of Burke Marshall [Assistant Attorney General]) and fear of violence among extreme elements - both Negro and white.

Still it sounds like a great, if limited, victory. King and Abernathy talk about massive Negro voter-registration drive beginning immediately, and say city government will have to face problem of school desegregation. Conference breaks up. Despite King mentioning God and historical occasion a lot, feel I've been witnessing history.

Pretty damn exciting.

# Press Conference Announcing the Birmingham Truce

Rev. Shuttlesworth, as head of ACMHR, opens the press conference and reads his prepared statement on the terms of the truce. Reporters prefer to speak with SCLC leader Rev. King who then reads his prepared remarks and fields questions from the reporters, even as an exhausted Shuttlesworth collapses and is carried from the scene. Local press accounts do not mention Shuttlesworth or his role in the settlement.

*Reverends King, Shuttlesworth and Abernathy (seated left to right) with reporters at the joint ACMHR-SCLC press conference to announce the Birmingham Truce, Courtyard, A. G. Gaston Motel, The Birmingham News Collection BPLDAM.*

# *Bombing, Rioting Across the City*

The Saturday evening following the Truce, bombs explode at the A. D. King House, the First Baptist Church of Ensley Parsonage, and at the A. G. Gaston Motel, the SCLC staff's Birmingham residence. Violence erupts into a situation which ACMHR historian Glenn Eskew describes as "the first urban riot of the 1960s."

"*A.D. King Home destroyed by 2 dynamite blasts in Ensley,*" The Birmingham News, May 12, 1963, page 1A, The Birmingham News *Collection BPLDAM 1076.1.88.*

*Police officers, firemen and an armored vehicle near burning houses, 15th Street, AP/Wide World Photoss, BPLDAM AP Collection 1076.1.44.*

# *Be Nonviolent*

Rev. King, Jr., returns to Birmingham (He terms it: "Bombingham") to assist local leaders in maintaining calm. In comments to the ACMHR, King urges restraint despite the bombings, threats, troops, tanks and water hoses. President Kennedy sends riot-control troops to state bases.

*He (Rev. King, Jr.) asked them to be calm; it is difficult to face in Birmingham what has happened through the years; but do the right way and we can win, but we can't win by meeting violence with violence. He said, 'There may be more blood to flow on the streets of Birmingham before we get our freedom, but let it be our blood instead of the blood of our white brother. The agreements that have been made will be met.* – Rev. Martin Luther King, Jr., quoted by Birmingham policemen: B. A. Allison, R. S. Whitehouse, R. A. Watkins, Mass Meeting, May 13, 1963, Sixth Avenue Baptist Church.

## Birmingham's Challenge For Peace and Order

Editorial, *Birmingham World*, May 15, 1963, Page 21.

In the wake of an apparent agreement made in Birmingham on the segregation front, there became a tragic aftermath which necessitated the standing by of troops just in case. Dynamiting and spurious activities of the Klan-minded, followed in rapid order, which betrayed the fact that extremism was still at work to the discredit of what had been attempted around conference tables.

Bombing and disorder set in early Sunday morning which made no contribution to what negotiators had attempted to settle.

Truly this is not the American way. No one in his late hour of advancement of our form and essence of Democracy would welcome such a disservice at a time when we can ill afford such adverse advertisement to the world.

The President of the United States deplored this outrage of violence and has appealed to both races in the Birmingham area to assist in the restoration of order and the peace. The President in addition, dispatched troops near the Birmingham area, hoping that they will not be needed. This surely can obtain if the people will cooperate and allow the law to take its course.

It is as simple as this: the courts have spoken; we live in a framework of laws and none should hold debatable that the laws of the land will be upheld.

Let sanity prevail: let every citizen come to himself and fully subscribe to our overall philosophy of respect for the laws of the land.

Birmingham — may we now have Peace?

# The New Frontier is trying to catch up with the Negro Frontier

Excerpts: Rev. Shuttlesworth's *A Little Closer to Freedom*, Annual Address to the ACMHR, Metropolitan A. M. E. Zion Church

My dear members and fellow citizens. After seven long years of hardship, danger, toil and struggle, we find ourselves being committed in such a way to the removal of segregation and sign barriers that Birmingham had become no longer a by-word of hate, malice and wicked racism; but the magic that strikes fire in people's hearts across this nation and the world. . . .

The eyes of the world have been focused on the spot; and somehow we are led to believe that because of the demonstration in Birmingham, Alabama, segregation will end in this country in a short time. . . . Little did we know seven years ago as we dared challenge this evil giant on these unchartered waters that we would celebrate our seventh anniversary in the history of a mass direct action campaign; and how glorious it is to realize that Negroes in Birmingham, Alabama, have not only helped to bring about a change in local government, but also a change in the attitude of the National Government about the racial situation.

Yes, my friends, the New Frontier is trying to catch up with the Negro frontier. Unless the President moves with dispatch, vigor and with a degree of dedication as that which was shown by Abraham Lincoln, Negroes will be demonstrating in every nook and cranny of the nation: north, east and west.

We are closer to freedom because the Negro in this city united as never before. Both young and old, students and adults, middle class, low class and no class, all joined together to put on the biggest mass demonstration ever to occur in America; and the economic boycott spoke its piece to the merchants that they, too, had to realize that this is a new day. Police dogs, the police lines and the water hoses could not put out the fire that started burning in Birmingham.

## Wallace Takes A Stand

Alabama Gov. George Wallace seeks to stop desegregation of the University of Alabama by blocking the registration of two black students accompanied by federal authorities.

# President John F. Kennedy Speaks to the Nation

The evening of Governor Wallace's schoolhouse door stand, President Kennedy goes on nationwide television to comment on Wallace's stance and to endorse the civil rights activism of Birmingham Blacks.

Excerpts: "President John F. Kennedy, Address to the Nation"

This nation was founded by men of many nations and backgrounds. It was founded on the principle that all men are created equal; and that the rights of every man are diminished when the rights of one man are threatened. . . .

And it ought to be possible for American citizens of any color to register and to vote in a free election without interference or fear of reprisal.

It ought to be possible, in short, for every American to enjoy the privileges of being American without regard to his race or his color.

This is not a sectional issue. Difficulties over segregation and discrimination exist in every city, in every state of the Union, producing in many cities a rising tide of discontent that threatens the public safety.

Nor is this a partisan issue. In a time of domestic crisis, men of goodwill and generosity should be able to unite regardless of party or politics.

This is not even a legal or legislative issue alone. It is better to settle these matters in the courts than on the streets, and new laws are needed at every level. But law alone cannot make men see right.

We are confronted primarily with a moral issue. It is as old as the Scriptures and is as clear as the American Constitution. The heart of the question is whether all Americans are to be afforded equal rights and equal opportunities; whether we are going to treat our fellow Americans as we want to be treated.

If an American, because his skin is dark, cannot eat lunch in a restaurant open to the public; if he cannot send his children to the best public schools available; if he cannot vote for the public officials who represent him; if, in short, he cannot enjoy the full and free life which all of us want, then who among us would be content to have the color of his skin changed and stand in his place?

Who among us would then be content with the counsels of patience and delay? One hundred years of delay have passed since President Lincoln freed the slaves, yet their heirs, their grandsons, are not fully free. They are not yet freed from the bonds of injustice; they are not yet freed from social and economic oppression.

And this nation, for all its hopes and all its boasts, will not be fully free until all its citizens are free.

Now the time has come for this nation to fulfill its promise. The events in Birmingham and elsewhere have so increased the cries for equality that no city or state or legislative body can prudently choose to ignore them.

The fires of frustration and discord are burning in every city, North and South. Where legal remedies are not at hand, redress is sought in the streets in demonstrations, parades and protests, which create tensions and threaten violence — and threaten lives.

We face, therefore, a moral crisis as a country and a people. It cannot be met by repressive police action. It cannot be left to increased demonstrations in the streets. It cannot be quieted by token moves or talk. It is a time to act in the Congress, in your state and local legislative body, and, above all, in all of our daily lives.

I am, therefore, asking the Congress to enact legislation giving all Americans the right to be served in facilities which are open to the public — hotels, restaurants and theaters, retail stores and similar establishments. This seems to me to be an elementary right.

I'm also asking Congress to authorize the Federal Government to participate more fully in lawsuits designed to end segregation in public education. We have succeeded in persuading many districts to desegregate voluntarily. Dozens have admitted Negroes without violence.

Other features will also be requested, including greater protection for the right to vote.

But legislation, I repeat, cannot solve this problem alone. It must be solved in the homes of every American in every community across our country.

In this respect, I want to pay tribute to those citizens, North and South, who've been working in their communities to make life better for all.

They are acting not out of a sense of legal duty but out of a sense of human decency. Like our soldiers and sailors in all parts of the world, they are meeting freedom's challenge on the firing line, and I salute them for their honor — their courage.

*"State Editors at White House- A group of Alabama editors and publishers (not pleased with President Kennedy's deployment of federal troops in Alabama) lunched with President Kennedy at the White House yesterday." The Birmingham News, UPI Telephoto. May 15, 1963, page 2.*

# *March on Washington*

Excerpts: Martin Luther King, Jr.'s "I Have A Dream" Speech. Reprinted with the permission of Martin Luther King, Jr., Center

So I say to you today, my friends, that even though we face the difficulties of today and tomorrow, I still have a dream. It is a dream deeply rooted in the American dream. I have a dream that one day this nation will rise up and live out the true meaning of its creed— "we hold these truths to be self-evident, that all men are created equal." I have a dream that one day on the red hills of Georgia, the sons of former slaves and the sons of former slave owners will be able to sit down together at the table of brotherhood. I have a dream that one day even the state of Mississippi, a state sweltering with the heat of injustice, sweltering with the heat of oppression, will be transformed into an oasis of freedom and justice. I have a dream my four little children will one day live in a nation where they will not be judged by the color of their skin, but by the content of their character.

I HAVE A DREAM TODAY!

I have a dream that one day down in Alabama—with its vicious racists, with its Governor having his lips dripping with the words of interposition and nullification—one day right there in Alabama, little black boys and black girls will be able to join hands with little white boys and white girls as sisters and brothers.

*In hopes that we could speak to the nation, the march was an effort to educate and move the nation to action to eliminate segregation, an effort to "Redeem the Soul of America" (SCLC's motto).* – Rev. Shuttlesworth, 1998.

*One of many demonstrations held across the United States during 1963 to show support for the Birmingham cause, San Francisco. People in Motion, 1966.*

# Schools Desegregate

Throughout the summer, Birmingham's Biracial Committee, appointed by Mayor Boutwell, labors to ensure peaceful compliance with court decisions to integrate schools and other public facilities. Meanwhile, Governor Wallace, other public officials and rabblerousers encourage protests and disregard for the law. School desegregation meets intense opposition.

*Shown entering Graymont School to register the first two Negro children to attend white public schools are, right to left, Rev. Shuttlesworth, Dwight Armstrong, Floyd Armstrong, James Armstrong, Birmingham Attorney Oscar Adams, Jr., and NAACP lawyer Constance Motley also accompanied the students. Dwight, 11, and Floyd, 10, enroll in the sixth and fifth grades at Graymont. Graymont School is in the Smithfield neighborhood. The Birmingham News, September 5, 1963, page 6.*

*"Bombing Sets Off Alabama Riot–Armed police block an intersection in Birmingham, Ala., to hold back a crowd of jeering Negroes. The mob congregated after the home of Negro attorney Arthur Shores was bombed for the second time in less than three weeks. Hundreds of screaming Negroes poured into the streets and started throwing bottles and rocks. One Negro was killed, one shot and several policemen were injured." Quentin Perry, Birmingham World, September 11, 1963, page 1. Arthur Shores's home is located on Center Street in a section of the Smithfield neighborhood, known as "Dynamite Hill," due to the numerous and unsolved bombings here. Attorney Arthur Shores, whose legal career spanned 50 years, successfully argued many of ACMHR's legal challenges. Birmingham World, September 11, 1963, page 1.*

## First Day of School

*Demonstrators, Phillips High School, September 12, 1963, The Birmingham News.*

Protesters at the city high schools—Phillips, West End and Woodlawn—carry signs and skirmish with city police.

## Ten Sticks of Dynamite
# Four Little Girls Dead

The dynamite blast at Sixteenth Street Baptist Church on Sunday morning, September 15, 1963, 10: 22 p.m. sounded an alarm heard round the world. Now, everyone could understand the atrocity and the hate that prevented desegregation.

*We must not harbor the desire to retaliate with violence. The deaths may well serve as the redemptive force that brings light to this dark city.* – Dr. Martin Luther King, Jr., at the funeral for three of the little girls whom he called "heroines of a holy crusade"

"*The 16th Street Baptist Church after a KKK bombing that killed four girls in a Sunday School class,*" *Danny Lyon, Magnum Photos, Inc., 1963.*

"*Officer with Bayonet Helps Maintain Order,*" *16th Street Baptist Church, Anthony Fairfield, The Birmingham News, September 16, 1963, page 7 .*

## Funeral of Three Little Girls

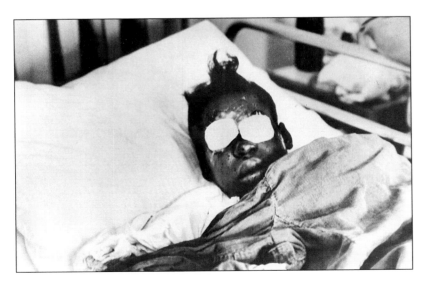

"Grandfather sobs. He lost loved one," Tom Langford, The Birmingham News, September 16, 1963, page 7.

Interior, Sixth Avenue Baptist Church, Funeral for Addie Mae Collins, 14; Denise McNair, 11; Cynthia Dianne Wesley, 14 , Rev. King is at the pulpit. Vernon Merritt, The Birmingham News, September 19, 1963, page 10. (Carole Rosamond Robertson, 14, was buried from St. John A.M. E. Church, the day before this funeral)

"Bomb Victim Funeral – Thousands of Negroes and many Whites surround the Sixth Avenue Baptist Church as pallbearers carry out a casket containing the body of one of four Negro children killed in a church bombing Sunday. A mass service for three of the victims drew one of the largest funeral crowds (2,000 inside, 4,000 outside) in Birmingham's history ." Birmingham Post-Herald, September 19, 1963, page 4.

Sara Jean Collins, September 15, 1963, Frank Danridge. This photograph is published as a two-page spread in Life Magazine, September 27, 1963. Sara Jean, Addie Mae Collins' sister, did not die in the bombing.

Demonstrations resume as city officials and merchants brake the agreements reached to end the spring demonstrations. Renewed Movement demonstrations — taking the form of pickets and marches— last for more than a year.

## NOVEMBER 26, 1963

# The Negro Revolution – Its Impact on American Life

Excerpts: Rev. Shuttlesworth's *National Guardian Dinner Speech,* Hotel Astor, NYC.

Let it suffice to say that the Negro in this country is through with Segregation and discrimination; and that this is clearly reflected in the nationwide protests and demonstrations of the Spring and Summer, and in the efforts at readjustments now being sought in all agencies of the federal and state governments, and in business enterprises around the country. It is also reflected in the record of the Court of the land, and now in the actions of religious bodies. . . . The issue is moral and spiritual as well as legal.

The Congress, in grappling with the C. R. legislation now understands that the issue is so grave that there can be no justice, no peace, no tranquility, no fulfillment of the promises, unless it acts. The Revolution has so moved America that in your day and mine, politicians will no longer climb and remain in office on the stairs of human poverty and enslavement.

In short, no facet of American life is untouched by the Revolution. . . .

## SPRING 1964

# Why We Can't Wait

Martin Luther King, Jr., publishes his account of the Birmingham campaign and urges reform in America's moral and political systems in *Why We Can't Wait-The moral leader of America eloquently states the case for Freedom now.*

# But for Birmingham

### The National Civil Rights Crisis and our Relationship to It

Excerpts Rev. Shuttlesworth's *Annual Address to the ACMHR,* 17th St. A.O.H. Church of God

Our goal is integration – the moral and brotherly acceptance of Negroes as human beings and citizens in the mainstream of American life – in Birmingham, in Alabama, and all over the United States. This is our National problem, America's gravest Crisis, and somehow Birmingham bears a peculiar and special relationship to it. It is true that the Negro drive started years ago by aiming at legal prohibitions against Segregation and Discrimination, and then in 1960 enlarged itself grasping at hamburgers and cups of coffee at public lunch counters. But we have long since surpassed this dimension.

Since the Birmingham Demonstrations of 1963, our nation has been in crisis, and its creaking and unequal social structure seeks to strike a balance between a maladjusted past and an uncertain future. At a July White House Conference, one of many racial meetings hastily summoned by President Kennedy in 1963, the President made the terse but profound statement: "But for Birmingham, we wouldn't be here today." What a tribute to be paid to your seven years of ordeal and hardship? What an acknowledgment that Birmingham, through the joint efforts of SCLC-ACMHR, had so stirred itself that it had shaken up the nation. How little did we know or even dream in 1956 that we would carry on and discipline ourselves as a Movement that destiny would use the Birmingham Movement as a vehicle to make America come to grips with its conscience! In this city, over 3,400 had filled the streets and overfilled the jails. Waterhoses tried in vain to drench a fire that wouldn't go out: dogs and police lines failed to stop the masses of young people and adults who meant it when they sang, "Ain't Gonna Let Nobody Turn Me Around." School children suddenly became freedom soldiers, and old men and women found themselves feeling young and useful again.

But for Birmingham! Sparks from Birmingham fell in Boston, New York, San Francisco, Houston, Texas, Chicago, Detroit and other cities were catching afire with the flames of freedom! The young and vigorous President saw that there would be open warfare and untold bloodshed unless he, as the Chief Officer of this so-called Christian Country, came up quickly with a law which would be a national expression of our supposedly moral order. Mr. Kennedy, with the voice of a modern prophet, told the nation via television that the issue was more a moral than legal one; and that we must cease being a nation of many creeds and few deeds.

But for Birmingham, the Civil Rights Bill would not be before Congress today! Let no one be deceived: It was neither church prayers nor conciliating committees which brought about the Civil Rights Bill. It was non-violent demonstrations, marching feet, praying hearts, singing lips and filling the jails which did it. Mr. Kennedy sensed the deep needs of the hour and sought to find a lasting remedy for the illness of his nation. . . .

In a real sense, ACMHR and the other Civil Rights Organizations of the country have given the Christian Church its greatest opportunity in centuries to make religion real in the lives of men. Thank God for the awakening of Religious forces!

But for Birmingham there would not be the agonizing reappraisal of the entire structure of the American system; a system which was planned without Negroes, built without Negroes-except for their unrequited labor, operated without Negroes, and designed to forever exist without Negroes being a part of its mainstream. It cannot be credited either to American goodness or an unexplainable accident that Negroes suddenly began appearing in T.V. movies and advertising media; and whoever heard of the cry. "Find qualified Negroes" in government, in business, and in industry? . . .

# ACMHR Accomplishments

Excerpts: *ACMHR Souvenir Booklet,* 1964.

One of the basic accomplishments is a solid sense of togetherness among Negroes - coupled with a disposition to protest the evils of segregation laws and practices. The Monday Night MASS MEETINGS have grown so that all churches accommodating them are overcrowded, and the spirit of dynamism with deep religious fervor pervades each meeting. The Movement is gaining friends and wide acceptance on every hand.

Although the organization always first seeks progress by petition and goodwill, it has been necessary to file many lawsuits.

Through the efforts of the Movement, 3,400 went to jail. ACMHR-SCLC massive demonstrations inspired the entire country. From those demonstrations and resultant uprisings all over the country, the Civil Rights Bill has passed the House and is now before the Senate.

The following places have been desegregated because of the Alabama Christian Movement for Human Rights: . . .

Expenditures for Bonds, Transcripts, Court Costs and Legal Fees have exceeded $128,574.16 in eight (8) years! From these figures alone one can see the dedication and determination of the Movement. . . .

Arrest, Jail and Harassments of many kinds have not dampened the spirit of the President, Officers, and Members of the ACMHR, and it can truthfully be said that "THE MOVEMENT IS MOVING" FOR "MORE IN '64!"

*The walls that were to preserve "segregation now, segregation forever,"are falling down flat, and in their places are rising gates which beckon onward the newer dimensions of 20th century idealism and racial progress. – ACMHR President's Message,* June 1964.

*Monday Night Mass Meeting, 17th Street A.O.H.Church of God, Bishop Roby, Pastor, May 18, 1964, ACMHR Souvenir Booklet, 1964, Lola Hendricks Collection.*

*ACMHR Usher Board. Seated left to right: Hattie Herndon, Harrison Bailey, Julia Rainge, Russell Conner, Fred DeBardeleben, John White and Herbert Palmer. Standing Front Row: Anglia Walker and Lisa Price. Standing second row, left to right: Loree Crenshaw, Sadie Roberts, Georgia Price, Rev. Edward Gardner, Florance Safford, Julia Fletcher and Rosa Walker. Third row, left to right: Availer Fowlkes, Tommie J. Hardy, Will Hall, Larry Walker, Eddie Burpo, Mack Roberson and Ben Owen. Members not shown: Roy Howard, Will Collins and Lenard Mays. ACMHR Annual Report 1964, Lola Hendricks Collection.*

*Executive Board: Standing Front Row: Mr. James Armstrong, Mrs. L. B. Robey, Rev. A. L. Woods, Jr., Rev. Edward Gardner, Rev. F. L. Shuttlesworth, Mrs. Georgia W. Price, Rev. L. J. Rogers, Mrs. Myrtis Dowdell, Mrs. Minnie Eaton. Second Row: Mrs. Dexter Brooks, Mr. J. J. Ryles, Rev. Calvin Woods. Third Row: Rev. Charles Billups, Rev. Soloman Crenshaw, Mr. James R. Revis, Mr. Lincoln Hendricks, Rev. C. H. George and Mr. E. H. Murphy. Members not shown: Mrs. Bradine King, Mrs. Lola Hendricks, Mr. George Price, Rev. N. H. Smith, Jr., Mrs. Daisy Jeffries; and Rev. A. D. Williams King. ACMHR Annual Report, 1964, Lola Hendricks Collection.*

# *President Lyndon Johnson signs Civil Rights Act of 1964.*

FEATURES
PICTURES
ARTICLES

# BIRMINGHAM WORLD
☆ A STANDARD RACE ☆ JOURNAL

A Newspaper With A Constructive Policy

VOLUME 32, NUMBER 69 — BIRMINGHAM, ALABAMA, WEDNESDAY, JULY 8, 1964 — PRICE TEN CENTS

DISCUSS MUSIC EVOLUTION — (L. to r.) Willie [...] lege in Atlanta; Dr. Zelma George, prominent lecturer on American Negro music and world affairs; and Dr. John A. Davis, President of the American Society of African Culture (AMSAC) and Chairman of the Department of Political Science at City College in New York City, as they engaged at the lecture-demonstration on "The Evolution of American Negro music from its African Roots" in Cleveland, Ohio, on June 20. The lecture-demonstration was part of AMSAC's Seventh Annual Meeting which was held at Karamu House in Cleveland, Ohio.

# RACIST BARRIERS TUMBLE

## President Signs House Passed Historic Laws

### By FRANK ELEAZER

WASHINGTON—(UPI)—Congress passed the civil rights bill Thursday and President Johnson signed it into the law of the land with a plea that all Americans join in this effort "to bring justice and hope to all of our people and to bring peace to our land."

The measure, born in the violence of the Negro protest movement against discrimination, completed its congressional journey around 2 p.m. EDT Thursday when the House passed it on a 289 to 126 vote.

The House action, stamping approval on the compromise version which had passed the Senate June 19, came one year and two weeks after the late President John F. Kennedy sent the bill to Congress.

Five hours later, in an impressive ceremony in the White House, Johnson put his signature to the bill. The proceedings including a 10-minute televised address to the nation by the President, were attended by senators, representatives, Cabinet members, and civil rights, religious and labor leaders.

### BILL A "CHALLENGE"

The President, in his address, said the bill is "a chalenge to all of us to go to work to eliminate the last vestiges of injustice in our beloved country."

He then announced a five -point program to implement the bill, starting with the appointment of former Florida Gov. Leroy Collins as head of the Community Relations Service.

Collins now is president of the National Association of Broadcasters.

The purpose of the Community Relations Service, established by the bill, is to conciliate racial disputes before the federal government would have to step in.

Johnson also said he would appoint a committee of distinguished Americans to help Collins.

### OTHER POINTS

The other three points he an-

(Continued on Page Six)

## Miles College Nears $200,000 Science Fund Grant

Miles College is $2,000 closer to its $200,000 Science Fund Campaign which moved off July 1.

Dr. L. H. Pitts, president of the college, announced that the Huber Foundation made a gift of $2,000 which is assigned to Science Fund Drive.

Dr. Pitts added:

"The drive will last through mid-August, and somehow Miles must get the other $190,000 so that construction on the science building can get underway."

"It is hoped that the entire country will awaken to the needs of a sruggling college which has great potential, but must have financial help in order to reach the academic horizons of higher education."

SCIENCE TEACHERS AT WORK — Vernon Clarke, standing, an instructor at North Carolina College's eighty Summer Science Institute for Teachers of Science and Mathematics, checks the work of two institute participants. Using microscopes are Gordon Postelwaite, Aurora, Ill., and Mrs. Dorothy Pate Jackson, Dublin, Ga. They are among 83 teachers from 11 states attending the National Science Foundation-sponsored institute.

## 10 Restaurants, 4 Theatres ABC Store Comply With U.S. Civil Rights Act Locally

At least 10 restaurants and four theatres, together with an ABC Store, let the spirit of the 1964 Civil Rights Act breathe through their operations in Birmingham, July 3.

Headquarters of the Alabama Christian Movement for Human Rights, of which the Rev. F. L. Shuttlesworth is president, revealed that the day following the signing the Act into law by President Lyndon B. Johnson compliance groups from the ACMHR tested the Act and were received courteously in several cafes and theaters which previously did not have the benefit of Negro trade.

A report meeting was held Friday night, July 3, at the New Pilgrim Baptist Church of which the Rev. N. H. Smith, Jr., ACMHR secretary, is the pastor. The Rev. Shuttlesworth delivered the main speech.

The Rev. J. L. Ware, president

of the Birmingham Baptist Ministers Conference and vice-chairman of the Group Relations Sub-Committee of the Birmingham Community Affairs Committee, according to the daily press, said that in his "personal opinion . . the local Negro community is grateful to the white citizens of Birmingham for their kindness and consideration."

In a joint statement, the Birmingham Hotel Assn. and the Birmigham Motel Assn. indicated that they would comply with the section of the Act which affected their business.

Mayor Albert Boutwell, in a cautious statement July 3 said that he had confidence that Birmingham leaders and citizens have the "ability to meet a critical situation with maturity and objectivity." He added that it is "far too early to assess the long range effects (of

the Act) on business and individual behavior."

There were no reports from civic leaders in the outlying cities and towns in Jefferson County regarding the way the Act was being accepted and implemented. Bessemer hotel and cafe operators were expected a statement July 6. In both Bessemer and Fairfield racial ordinances have been removed from their governing codes.

In the ABC Store at 14th St. and 5th Ave., No., there were reports that Negro customers ignored the racial lines. However, in Ensley it is said that one whiskey store Negro whiskey buyers were standing in a long Jim Crow line.

In a statement signed by the Rev. Shuttlesworth and Dr. Edward Gardner, first vice-president, the ACHMR said:

"The Civil Rights Bill really means the second Emancipation of the American Negro. It gives the Negro equal status with other Americans, and gives him the right to challenge in court any discrimination practiced against him."

"Negroes have suffered long and hard to bring this day to pass; and now they rejoice with all other freedom loving citizens that American democracy has at long last itself. Our rejoicing must be tempered however, with the understanding of the hardships, the sufferings, the bombings, and even the deaths of many of our people in many places. Such knowledge

## Collins Outlines CRS Rights Law Objectives

WASHINGTON — (UPI) — Replacing bitterness with fairness and cooperation will be the primary aim of the new federal civil rights meditation agency, its director-designate Leroy Collins said Friday.

Atty. ARTHUR D. SHORES — L. S. GAILLARD, JR.

## Shores, Gallard Picked

## Nyasaland Now Independent

BLANTYRE, Nyasaland — (UPI) — Formal celebrations leading to the creation of Africa's newest independent state began Sat. in this tiny land of poverty, disease and ignorance.

At the stroke of midnight Sunday, Nyasaland will be declared free of British rule and become Malawi, the 37th independent republic of Africa.

In advance of Sunday's ceremony, pictures of the first prime minister, Dr. Hastings Banda, were posted in most stores.

Banda began the independence festivities by opening the country's first trade fair at Limbe. Goods from the United States, Britain, West Germany and Portugal were displayed in more than 100 booths.

Eighty nations are sending diplomatic representatives for Sunday's ceremony.

## AROUND THE TOWN

IN THE WIND

The Jefferson County Progressive Democratic Council is sche-

## WHAT NEW CIVIL RIGHTS ACT COVERS

1. Hotels, motels and other places affording lodging to transient guests
2. Restaurants, lunch counters, soda fountains, cafeterias, and other places selling food to the public.
3. Theaters, movie houses, concert halls, sports arenas, stadiums, and other places of entertainment and exhibition
4. Gasoline station rest rooms and facilities.
5. Businesses located in or which contain a service or facility as listed above.
6. Any place of public accommodation in which "discrimination or segregation is or purports to be required by any law, statute, ordinance, regulation, rule or order of a State or any agency or political subdivision thereof."

homes.

6. The professional services of doctors, lawyers, dentists, and others licensed by the city, county, or State.

7. Persons improperly dressed, drunk, or disorderly.

WHAT INDIVIDUAL CAN DO IF REFUSED SERVICE

(Test in small numbers, be properly dressed and do not use force. Give law a chance.)

1. Notify the United States District Attorney, Atlanta Leadership Conference, NAACP, Greater Atlanta Council on Human Relations, or Civil Rights Commission in Washington, D. C.

2. File lawsuit in a Federal court; or the Department of Justice may enter the case and file the suit in the name of the United States.

a. Federal judge may wish to refer case to Community Relations Service for voluntary compliance before processing a suit.

b. If court finds law has been violated, the offender must pay your court costs

c. Neither criminal penalties nor the recovery of money damages are permissible under the law.

WHAT ACT DOES NOT COVER

1. Hotels, motels, or lodging houses which have less than six rooms and in which the proprietor makes his home

2. Private clubs which operate in "good faith"

3. Retail stores, unless they also operate as a restaurant

4. Barber shops, beauty parlors, and other service facilities

# The Nation Will Never Forget What We Did Together

*Finally the Civil Rights Bill passed. Because the people of Birmingham were already in motion they were able to make this the first city in the South to have mass tests of the new law.*

– Anne Braden, Birmingham, *People in Motion,* 1966.

Miss Notie B. Andrews, describes the first tests:

*After the Civil Rights Bill was passed, everybody knew we were going to town that morning. All the news folks in town were there–looked like everybody was there. We had a news conference and then we hit the streets.*

*Around two o'clock we went to all the restaurants and theaters downtown and stayed there all afternoon. Where I went, they were real nice. The other people were staring at us to see how we would react, but we acted just like they weren't there. . . . After that every day for about two weeks we would send a different group of people, in order to let them know we really meant that we were going to come in.*

— Miss Notie B. Andrews, *People in Motion,* 1966.

---

Excerpts: Rev. Fred Shuttlesworth, Annual Address, June 5, 1965, Municipal Auditorium.

Let it never be forgotten that ACMHR, together with SCLC, provided the vehicle and shock force that shook this nation's moral conscience in 1963 as never before, resulting in the Civil Rights Bill which will ultimately cause all facets of our society to reevaluate and adjust to the demands of the 20th Century. These 1963 Birmingham demonstrations laid the foundation for the superb and magnificent Selma Demonstrations of 1965 (in which ACMHR played a full and effective role) during which the moral conscience of the land was again stirred until very soon the Nation will be fully committed morally and legally to complete support of the concept of full human dignity, justice and freedom.

Excerpts: Rev. Fred Shuttlesworth, *Tenth Annual Address to the Alabama Christian Movement for Human Rights,* 1966, A. O. H. Cathedral.

But God has his purposes, time brings about a change, and human beings who are genuinely committed to righteousness and justice make a difference. Have you forgotten June 5, 1956? When Alabama outlawed the National Association for the Advancement of Colored People, we Negroes arose by hundreds and by thousands to declare that "they may outlaw an Organization but they cannot outlaw a people determined to be free." We committed ourselves to non-violence and love, declaring that we Negroes would not "harm the hair on the head of one white person" in our struggle to be free. We vowed to pray for those who despitefully used us, and to keep on loving those who kept on acting as if they hated us.

We struggled alone in the pitch blackness from 1956 until the sixties came on. We had legally challenged all forms and areas of segregation here in Birmingham, and were cooperating with other local and National groups insofar as we could. The coming of the Sit-ins and Freedom Rides involved us even more in the national destiny of America. Our legal entanglements paved the way for *TIME* Magazine to write in November 1965 that your President had achieved the distinction of having fought and won more cases than any other man in the history of the U. S. Supreme Court.

Some men may little note nor long remember what we say here; but the Nation will never forget what we did together. We were not satisfied with the few scattering cracks in the Segregation wall, and decided to effect a major confrontation with evil. Joining with the Southern Christian Leadership Conference, led on by illustrious Martin Luther King, Jr., Negroes filled the jailhouses and streets of Birmingham in 1963 until the White House became concerned about the poor houses in America, and the man of destiny in the White House became an ally of the black men in the streets of Birmingham. We "shook up" the Country and made America conscious of its morality and commitment to the ideals of justice and humanitarianism. The late President Kennedy, God rest his soul and fulfill his vision, opened one of the many hurriedly called White House conferences on the Civil Rights Act of 1964 with the classic and caustic remark of: "Gentlemen, but for Birmingham and what happened there, we would not be here today."

Birmingham really caused the Federal Government to begin having genuine and legitimate overt concern about the Freedom of Negroes. The 1964 Civil Rights Bill expresses legitimate concern and interest in many areas of human existence – schools, hotels, public accommodations and job opportunities. The Voting Act of 1966, coming after the Selma Demonstration was really an extension and further dimension of what happened here.

# Civil Rights Era Churches Information Summary

This list of Birmingham churches includes: 1963 & 1998 church names, dates of establishment, date(s) of construction of the Civil Rights era churches, 1963 addresses as listed in the Birmingham & Bessemer city directories, Civil Rights era pastor(s); 1998 Addresses, 1998 Pastors; Jefferson County tax identification numbers and date(s)of tax assessor photographs & credits for other photographs appearing in *A Walk to Freedom*. Asteriks * indicate that the Civil Rights era church remains. When several tax photographs exist double asteriks ** indicate photographs used in this publication. All tax assessor photographs may be purchased from the Birmingham Public Library Department of Archives and Manuscripts. Please notify the Society if records exist showing the use of other Birmingham area churches for meetings.

1. *Abyssinia Baptist Church, est. 1929 (1951) 1501 Avenue L, Ensley, Rev. Louree R. Jackson (1952-1964); 1501 Avenue L, Ensley, Rev. R. L. Patterson; tax # 22-31-4-24-1, tax photographs: 12/18/39-5/7/64**.

2. *Bethel A.M.E. Church, est. 1888 (1942, 1955) 1524 Avenue D, Ensley, Rev. Floyd E. Legg (c.1956-c.1960), Rev. Edward Mixon (1961-1973); 1524 Avenue D, Rev. Ronald Nored; tax # 22-31-2-10-7, tax photograph: 12/02/54.

3. *Bethel Baptist Church, est. 1904 (1926) 3191 29th Avenue North, Collegeville, Rev. Fred L. Shuttlesworth (1953-1961), Rev. Vincent C. Provitt (1961-1974); 3191 29th Avenue North & 3200 28th Avenue North, Rev. Thomas Wilder, Jr.; tax # 22-13-4-33-1, tax photograph: 01/04/33.

4. *Canaan (Missionary) Baptist Church, est. 1865 (1961) 1429 9th Avenue West Bessemer, Rev. John H. Browder (1951- c.1963); 824 15th Street North, Rev. Horace P. Turner; tax # 38-9-2-28-1, tax photographs: 3/16/40 & 01/16/45*. (The photograph published is not the Movement-era structure.)

5. *Christian Valley Baptist Church, est. by 1914 (1914+) 3104 33rd Terrace North Birmingham, Rev. A. Lawrence Lawson (1957-1965); 3104 33rd Terrace North, Rev. Herbert Benson; tax # 22-13-2-21-6, tax photograph: 01/18/61.

6. *East End Baptist Church, est. 1919 (1947) 2609 Sixth Avenue South, Southside, Rev. Calvin Woods (1958-1974); 2609 6th Avenue South, Rev. Johnny L. Mosby; tax # 23-31-3-13-3, tax photograph: 11/12/47;Pastor active in ACMHR; churches too small for meetings.

7. *First Baptist Church, East Thomas, est. 1938 (c.1946) 419 11th Court West, East Thomas, Rev. John A. Hayes (1942-1970); 419 11th Court West, Rev. Johnnie Howze; tax # 22-27-3-18-3, tax photograph: 04/15/46, photograph courtesy: First Baptist Church, Joseph T. Moore.

8. First Baptist Church, Ensley, est. 1900 (1926) 1534 19th Street, Ensley, Rev. Wesley H. Thomas(1934-Oct.1956,evening First Baptist Ensley hosted its first ACXMHR meeting), Rev. Walter L. Little (1960-1961), Rev. Alfred D. Williams King (1963-1964); 1508 19th Street, Rev. Thomas E. Gilmore; tax # 22-31-4-32-9 A & B, tax photograph: 04/29/64** & 12/20/39**.

9. *First Baptist Church, Hooper City, est. 1925 (1946) 468 37th Court West, Hooper City, Rev. James E. Townsend (c.1961-1964); 452 37th Court West, Rev. Walker; tax # 22-15-3-14-11 A & B, tax photograph: 11/04/48.

10. *First Baptist Church, Kingston, est. 1930 (c.1952) 4600 9th Avenue North, Kingston, Rev. George W. Dickerson (1941-1972); 4600 9th Avenue North, Rev. Nelson Miller; tax # 23-20-4-8-3, tax photograph: 08/15/52.

11. First Baptist Church, Woodlawn, est. 1931 (1945) 301 62nd Street South, Woodlawn, Rev. Frank Percy Huggins (1956-1967); 251 48th Street North, Rev. Odie Hoover III; tax # 23-22-2-34-4, tax photographs: 11/14/38 & 05/23/62**.

12. *First Ebenezer Baptist Church, est. 1941 (1942) 420 Graymont Avenue West, Smithfield, Rev. Oscar W. Holliday (1949-1959), Rev. John F. Hardy (1952-1981); 420 Graymont Avenue West, Rev. Robert Dawson; tax # 22-35-3-11-13, no tax photograph, photograph: Birmingham Historical Society field photograph, 1998.

13. First Metropolitan Baptist Church (c.1936) 2523 Fourth Avenue South, Southside, Rev. Abraham L. Woods, Jr. (1956-1966); church currently building a new campus, Rev. Henry Hicks; tax # 23-31-3-25-1, tax photograph: 01/20/39.

14. Forty-Sixth Street Baptist Church, est. 1914 (1956) 1532 Cahaba Street, E. Birmingham, Rev. Richard S. Brown (1963-c.1965); 230 85th Street North, Rev. Fredrick Whitt; tax # 23-19-1-5-25, tax photograph: 04/19/62.

15. *Galilee Baptist Church, est. 1918 (1920) 1013 23rd Street North, Northside, Rev. Richard H. Thompkins (1952-1975); historic church currently abandoned, 1231 24th Street North, Rev. Dr. Samuel L. Matt; tax # 22-25-3-4-2, tax photograph: 02/02/61.

16. Groveland Baptist Church, est. 1905 (1910) 452 66th Street North, Woodlawn, Rev. Oscar W. Holliday (1960-1990); 5337 Fifth Ave. S., Rev. E. B. Burpo; no tax record, photograph: Groveland Baptist Church, Annette Short.

17. *Hopewell Baptist Church, est. 1929 (1941,1959) 2315 26th Avenue North, ACIPCO, Rev. Lonnie S. Thomas (c.1946-1963), Rev. Jesse Brown (1964-1981); 2315 26th Avenue North, Rev. Timothy J. Woods, Sr.; tax # 22-23-1-38-3, tax photograph: 10/28/59.

18. Jackson Street Baptist Church, est. 1890 (1904) 230 63rd Street South, Woodlawn, Rev. Joseph C. Parker (c.1959-1975); 309 63rd Street South, Rev. Gregory Hollis; tax # 23-22-2-31-22, tax photographs: 11/13/38** & 6/13/62.

19. Lily Grove Baptist Church, est. 1927 (1934) 1015 3rd Street North, Druid Hills, Rev. Ambus Hill (1963-c.1991); 1409 20th North, Druid Hills, Rev. Don Solomon; tax # 22-34-1-10-4, tax photograph: 04/04/47**.

20. Macedonia 17th Street Baptist Church, est. 1885 (1919) 922 17th Street North, Northside, Rev. Otis J. Jackson (1947-1965), Rev. Arnold D. Blackmon (1965-1994); 1405 13th Avenue North, Rev. Thomas Hunter; tax # 22-26-4-16-13, tax photograph: 02/19/39.

21. *Metropolitan A.M.E. Zion Church, est. 1885 (1903,1955) 1530 Fourth Avenue North, Northside, Rev. George W. McMurray (1952-1964); 1530 Fourth Avenue North, Rev. Dr. G. Ray Coleman; tax # 22-35-1-12-6, tax photograph: 09/24/56.

22. *Metropolitan C.M.E. Church, est. 1900 (1918,1939) 1733 18th Street, Ensley, Rev. Abraham J. Hicks (1950s), Rev. Clarence C. Cowsen (1953-1963); Christ Temple A.F.M. Church of God now occupying historic church, 1600-4 Avenue K, Ensley, Rev. Hattie D. Loving; tax # 22-31-4-33-4, tax photograph: 12/20/39.

23. *Metropolitan Community Church, est. 1938 (1946) 335 64th Street South, Woodlawn, Rev. Roosevelt Grier (c.1963-c.1965); 335 64th Street South, Rev. Carl Davis; tax # 23-22-2-26-1, tax photograph: 03/20/53.

24. *Mt. Ararat Baptist Church, est. 1914 (1916, 1950) 1920 Slayden Avenue, Sherman Heights, Rev. John H. Glover (c.1952-1965); 1920 Slayden Avenue, Rev. Albert Bry; tax # 21-36-1-17-1 A & B, tax photographs: 4/3/40 & 11/30/64**.

25. Mt. Olive Baptist Church, est. 1922 (by 1958) 6300 Third Avenue North, Woodlawn, Rev. Edward Gardner (1949-present); 2615 Fifth Avenue South, Rev. Anthony Hall; no tax record, photograph: ACMHR *Souvenir Booklet, 1958;* Pastor active in ACMHR; churches too small for meetings.

26. *New Bethlehem Baptist Church, est. 1901 (1953) 1730 11th Avenue North, Bessemer, Rev. James F. Steel (c.1951-c.1963); 1730 11th Avenue North, Rev. William Walker; tax # 38-4-3-18-11, tax photograph: 04/06/54.

27. New Hope Baptist Church, est. 1892 (1912) 3431 Second Avenue North, Avondale, Rev. Herman Stone (1947-1985); 1740 Cleburn Avenue SW, Rev. Gregory L. Clarke; tax # 23-30-4-7-1, tax photograph: 06/18/47.

28. *New Pilgrim Baptist Church, est. 1900 (1945,1959) 903 Sixth Avenue South, Southside, Rev. Nelson H. Smith Jr. (1954-present) Rev. Charles Billups, Jr. (Asst. to pastor, 1960s); 708 Goldwire Place SW, Rev. Dr. N. H. Smith, Jr.; tax # 29-2-1-11-2, tax photographs: 11/14/46 & 10/09/64**.

29. *New Rising Star Baptist Church, est. 1958 (1960s) 3104 33rd Place North, Collegeville, Rev. George E. Pruitt (1958-1986); 3104 33rd Place North, Rev. George E. Pruitt, Jr.; tax # 22-13-4-13-11, tax photograph: 10/04/68; pastor active in ACMHR; too small for meetings.

30. New Salem Baptist Church, est. by 1919 (1920s) 1632 6th Street North, ACIPCO, Rev. Henry S. Freeman (c.1959-1965); 1632 6th Street North, Rev. Stanley Hall; tax # 22-26-2-21-17, tax photograph: 02/19/39.

31. *Oak Street Baptist Church, est. 1916 (1961) 3224 Virginia Ave., Collegeville, Rev. Charles L. Vincent (1952-1958); 3224 Virginia Avenue, Rev. C. M. Murdock; tax # 22-13-1-19-7, tax photograph: 11/29/61.

32. *(Sixth Street) Peace Baptist Church (1948) 302 Sixth Street North, Northside, Rev. John H. Stenson (1947-1969); 302 Sixth Street North, Rev. Hobdy Moorer, Jr.; tax # 22-35-3-41-10, photograph courtesy Sixth Street Peace Baptist Church, Rev. Moorer.

33. Pleasant Grove Baptist Church, est. 1902 (1926,1964) 14 37th Street, Fairfield, Rev. Rector E. Avery (c.1960s-1994); 401 52nd Street, Fairfield, Rev. Willie Wells; no tax record, photograph: Pleasant Grove Baptist Church.

34. Regular (St. Matthew) Missionary Baptist Church, est. 1943 (1945) 1205 Cahaba Street, E. Birmingham, Rev. Charles H. George (1944-1972); 868 44th Street North, Kingston, Rev. Larry McCree, Jr.; tax # 23-19-1-19-13, tax photograph: 01/24/47, photograph: St. Matthew Missionary Baptist Church, Rev. McCree, Jr.

35. St. James Baptist Church, est. by 1893 (1914) 1100 6th Avenue North, Northside, Rev. Marzett L. Thornton (1922-1964); 1300 24th Street North, Rev. Gerald Jones; tax # 22-35-1-35-13, photograph courtesy *The Birmingham News Collection,* Birmingham Public Library Department of Archives and Manuscripts.

36. St. John A.M.E. Church, est. 1873 (1925-1942) 1430 7th Avenue North, Northside, Rev. Bishop Cornelius E. Thomas (c.1956-1965); 708 15th Street North, Rev. Karnie C. Smith; tax # 22-35-1-18-12, tax photographs: 2/24/39 & 12/12/66**.

37. *St. John Baptist Church, est. by 1910 (1910,1966) 2401 Carlos Avenue SW, Powderly, Rev. Joseph C. Crosby (1949-c.1960s), Rev. Ambus Hill (1956-1962), Rev. J. S. McMurray; 2401 Carlos Avenue, Rev. Morris Perry; tax # 29-17-3-30-1, tax photographs: 2/24/39 & 12/12/66**.

38. *St. Luke A.M.E. Church, est. 1893 (1926) 2803 21st Avenue North, N. Birmingham, Rev. Andrew W. Thomas (1956-1969); 2801 21st Avenue North; tax # 22-24-2-18-1, tax photograph: 01/31/39.

39. *St. Luke A.M.E. Zion Church, est. 1888 (1930) 3937 12th Avenue North, E. Birmingham, Rev. John O. Hart (1960-1963); 3937 12th Avenue North, Rev. Leonard Cammack; tax # 23-19-1-20-3, tax photograph: 01/14/39**; photograph courtesy: Constance Moore.

40. St. Paul A.M.E. Church, est. by 1911 (by 1948) 300 4th Court North, Smithfield, Rev. Samuel M. Davis(1959-1986); building a new church across the street from the historic site, Rev. C. C. Cummings; tax # 22-34-4-25-4, tax photograph: 01/22/48.

41. St. Paul C.M.E. Church, est. 1916 (1910s) 400 Circle Street, Docena, Civil Rights era pastor unknown; 400 Circle Drive; tax # 21-14-2-1-2, tax photograph: 09/08/52.

42. *St. Paul (United) Methodist Church, est. 1869 (1925,1950) 1500 Sixth Avenue North, Northside, Rev. Jacob C. Wilson (1954-1962), Rev. Otis R. Flournsy (1963-1964), Rev. Joseph E. Lowery (1965-1969); 1500 Sixth Avenue North, Rev. Frank J. Lee; tax # 22-35-1-10-12, tax photograph: 01/20/49.

43. *St. Peter Primitive Baptist Church, est. 1911 (1943) 2115 Fourth Avenue, Bessemer, Rev. William A. Clark (c.1946-1962); 2115 Fourth Avenue, Bessemer, Rev. Solomon Oliver; tax # 38-10-2-5-5, tax photograph: 04/21/40.

44. *(Old) Sardis Baptist Church, est. 1884 (1920s) 1240 4th Street North, Enon Ridge, Rev. Robert Louis Alford (1950-1971); 1240 Fourth Street North, Rev. Willie Smith; tax # 22-26-3-19-15, tax photograph: 03/03/39.

45. Seventeenth Street A.O.H. (AOH Cathedral), est. 1942 (1904) 630 17th Street North, Northside, Rev. Bishop Jasper Roby (1953-present); 1120 24th Street, North, Bishop Jasper Roby; tax # 22-35-1-4-1, tax photograph: 03/01/39.

46. *Shady Grove Baptist Church, est. 1902 (1943) 3444 31st Way North, Collegeville, Rev. Lewis J. Rogers (1949-1995); 3444 31st Way North, Rev. Michael Yarbrough; tax # 22-13-1-16-22 A & B, tax photograph: 05/05/76; pastor active in ACMHR; church too small for meetings.

47. *Sixteenth Street Baptist Church, est. 1873 (1909-1911) 1530 Sixth Avenue North, Northside, Rev. John Cross (1962-1968); 1530 Sixth Avenue North, Rev. Christopher Hamlin; tax # 22-35-1-10-13, tax photograph: 03/01/39.

48. Sixth Avenue Baptist Church, est. 1881 (1910) 1529 Sixth Avenue, South, Southside, Rev. John Thomas Porter (1963-present); 1101 Martin Luther King, Jr. Drive, Rev. John Thomas Porter; no tax record, photograph: Birmingham View Company, 1924, with negative at Birmingham Public Library Department of Archives and Manuscripts.

49. *(Sixth Avenue) Zion Hill Baptist Church (1958) 1414 Sixth Avenue North, Northside, Rev. Melvin B. Goodwin (1947-1970); Deliverance Temple Inter-Faith Church now uses historic church; tax # 22-35-1-17-12, tax photograph: 07/08/60.

50. *South Elyton Baptist Church, est. 1914 (1940-47) 102 First Street South, Southside, Rev. A. Moreland Lanier (1951-1977); historic church used for Sunday school and community meetings, 100 First Street South, Rev. Reginald Brown; tax # 29-3-4-13-1, tax photograph: 09/10/64.

51. *Starlight Baptist Church, est. by 1910s (1910s) 1280 AL 150, Muscoda, Rev. Asbury Howard; 1280 Highway 15, Rev. Williams, Bessemer; tax # 38-15-4-8-2, Birmingham Historical Society field photograph, 1998.

52. Tabernacle Baptist Church, est. 1886, 1013 25th Street North,   Northside, Rev. Joseph H. Calloway (1959-1963); 600 Center Street North, Rev. Edsel M. Davis, Sr.; no tax record, photograph courtesy Tabernacle Baptist Church, Benny East; Mrs. Gilmore Dinkins, photographer.

53. Thirgood (Memorial) C.M.E. Church, est. c.1879 (c.1953) 1027 Seventh Avenue, North, Northside, Moses C. Merriweather (1961-1962), Rev. Nathaniel Linsey (1963-1967); 517 Center Street North, Rev. R. R. Summerville; no tax record. photograph courtesy: Mrs. Ceola Montgomery.

54. *Thirty-Second Street Baptist Church, est. 1910 (1924) 518 32nd Street, South, Southside, Rev. Charles H. Parker (1949-1983); new congregation occupying the historic church, 3012 Dowell Avenue, SW, Rev. Roy Chester Allen; tax # 23-31-1-35-12, tax photograph: 01/12/39.

55. *Twenty-Second Ave. Baptist Church, est. 1878 (1917,1960) 2614 22nd Avenue North, N. Birmingham, Rev. I. Clifton Ravizee (c.1959-1991); 2614 22nd Avenue North, Rev. Zachary Operton; tax # 22-24-2-8-3 A & B, tax photograph: 04/03/64.

56. Union Bethel Independent Methodist Church, est. 1932 (1952) 1300 Sixth Avenue South, Southside, Rev. Terry L. Lane Sr.(1953-1962), Rev. Roosevelt Grier (1959); 1912 14th Street SW, Rev. Kenneth Robinson; no tax record, photograph: ACMHR *Souvenir Booklet, 1958.*

57. *West End Hills Baptist Church, est. 1921 (1965) 1700 19th Place SW, West End, Rev. Coleman M. Smith (c.1959-1965); 1680 19th Place SW, Rev. Wilmer Jackson; tax # 29-17-4-11-1, tax photograph: 07/11/51.

58. *Zion Spring Baptist Church, est. 1927 (1948) 528 41st Street North, Kingston, Rev. Elmer J. Minnifield (c.1946-c.1967); 528 41st Street North, Rev. George Johnson; tax # 23-29-2-4-26, tax photograph: 03/31/60.

59. Zion Star Baptist Church, est. 1913, 2611 Fourth Avenue South Southside, Rev. James S. Phifer (1954-1963), Rev. Joseph Calloway (1964-present); 254 Third Avenue SW, Rev. J. H. Calloway; tax # 23-31-2-32-2, tax photograph: 05/16/57, photograph courtesy: *ACMHR Souvenir Booklet,* 1958.

60. *First Congregational (Christian) Church (UCC), est. 1882 (1953) 1022 Center, North Smithfield, Rev. Harold D. Long (1956-1970); 1024 Center Street North, Rev. Dr. Rodney Franklin; tax # 22-34-1-14-1, tax photographs: 03/05/53** & 9/17/64.

## Churches Purchasing Advertisements for the ACMHR Souvenir Booklets, 1964 & 1965

Broad Street Missionary Baptist Church
Church of God in Christ
Enon Methodist Church
Faith Followers Church of Trust
Fifth Street Church of God
First Baptist Church of College Heights, Inc., Zion City
First Baptist Church of Pratt City
First Baptist Church of Zion City
Greater New Antioch Baptist Church
Greater Temple Baptist Church
Mount Olive Baptist Church
Mount Sinai Missionary Baptist Church
New Peace Baptist Church
New Progress Baptist Church
Our Lady of Fatima Catholic Church
St. Joseph Baptist Church
St. Mark C. M. E. Church
St. Matthews Baptist Church
Shady Grove Baptist Church and
Twenty-Third Street Baptist Church.

*Some ministers were members of the ACMHR, however, their churches were too small to accommodate the ACMHR meetings. Other ministers that were not with the ACMHR had members of the ACMHR. The members would solicit ads from their churches. Meetings were held at some of the Ad purchasers listed above.*

-Yvonne Turner, ACMHR Program Chairman 1964 & Fundraiser

# Acknowledgments

The creation and publishing of this volume has been assisted by a very large number of individuals. What follows is a list of many who have helped.

**Financial Assistance**

For the publication:

Birmingham Historical Society

For support of the accompanying photographic exhibition at the Birmingham Public Library:

November 1, 1998-December 31, 1998

Birmingham Public Library, Jack Bulow, Director; Anne Knight, Coordinator of Research Services; Sharon Hill, Head of Public Relations; Frank Golden, Building Services; Leroy Mauldin, Gallery Coordinator.

Alabama Humanities Foundation: Robert Stewart, Director; Marion Carter, Project Liason

Anonymous Donors.

For support of the accompanying Symposium: *Birmingham Revolutionaries: The Rev. Fred Lee Shuttlesworth and the Alabama Christian Movement for Human Rights* with participants including the Rev. Shuttlesworth, Rev.Wilson Fallin, Jr. , Rev. Wyatt Tee Walker, Glenn Eskew, Andrew Manis and Aldon Morris, held at the Sixteenth Street Baptist Church, November 1, 1998:

And for the support of the old-fashioned Mass Meeting, Monday, November 1, 1998, held at the Bethel Baptist Church, Collegeville:

The Alabama Humanities Foundation: Robert Stewart, Director; Marion Carter, Project Liason

Anonymous Donors.

**Production**

Design & Production: Scott Fuller, icon graphics

*Copy Editors*: Lela Anne Brewer; Stewart Dansby; Rhonda Dowling; James W. Emison; William Gresham; Edgar Marx, Sr.; Joseph Strickland; James H. White III; Steve Yoder.

*Readers & Advisors*: Stewart Dansby; Wilson Fallin, Jr.; Lola Hendricks; Rev. Fred L. Shuttlesworth; James H. White III; Dr. Marvin Whiting; Rev. Abraham Woods, Jr.; Odessa Woolfolk.

*Researchers*: Lauren Bishop; Michelle Crunk; Karyn Emison; Amy Hamilton; Brenda Howell; Alicia McGivaren, Michelle Morgan; Alison Ray; Fred Renneker IV; Marjorie Lee White; Marjorie L. White, *Research Director*.

*Birmingham Public Library Department of Archives and Manuscripts, Microfilm, Public Relations, Social Sciences and Tutwiler Collection of Southern History Staffs for assistance with the use of the library's extensive Civil Rights collections and for hosting the* A Walk to Freedom *exhibition*: Jim Baggett; John Corley; Yvonne Crumpler; Sharon Hill; Anne Knight; LaSundra Murphy; Dennis Nichols; Rodney Porterfield; Yolanda Valentin; Don Veasey; Sherri Washington.

*Birmingham Civil Rights Institute Staff:* Wayne Coleman; Florence Wilson Davis; Lola Hendricks; Eric Watson; Odessa Woolfolk, President; Lawrence Pigeaux, Director.

*For assistance with photographs, church histories and other information*: The 60 Movement Churches, their pastors and church secretaries; Robert Adams; Vivian Corey, *Greater New Light Baptist Church, Cincinnati, Ohio*; Dr. Jack Davis; Reuben Davis; Benny East, Rev. Erskine Faush; Lillie M. H. Fincher; Sara Fuller; Doris Gary; Irene P. George; Lola Hendricks; Hezekiah Jackson IV; Col. Stone Johnson; Queen Pruitt McArthur; Angela S. Mondy; Mrs. Ceola Montgomery; Constance Moore; Joseph T. Moore; W. C. Motley; Carlton Reese; Rev. George E. Pruitt, Jr., Queen Pruitt McArthur, Anetta Pruitt Moore, Mrs. Sadie Mae Pruitt; Jeannetta Pruitt Woods; Annette Short; Yvonne W. Turner; Stella White; Rev. Thomas Wilder, Jr., Reuben Davis, Aldrich Gunn and Barbara Hightower;Norman B. Wooding, Jr.; and Marion Woods.

*Coordinating Committee for publication assistance and planning for the associated Movement-era Mass Meeting:* Reuben Davis, Aldrich Gunn, Rev. Christopher Hamlin, Lola Hendricks, Colonel Stone Johnson, Carlton Reese, Rev. Fred Shuttlesworth, Odessa Wolfolk, Rev. Abraham Woods with the assistance of the Bethel Baptist Church and Rev. Thomas Wilder.

*Public Relations Committee*: Wayne Coleman; Stewart Dansby; Florence Wilson Davis; Karyn Emison; Sara Fuller; Lola Hendricks; Sharon Hill; Felycia Jarrell; Carolanne Roberts; James H. Strickland; Marjorie L. White; Odessa Woolfolk.

# Grateful acknowledgment is made for permission to reprint the following excerpts and photographs:

Rev. Fred Lee Shuttlesworth's Annual Reports and Speeches to the ACMHR and other organizations and other ACMHR documents, Reprinted by permission of Rev. Fred Lee Shuttlesworth and Lola Hendricks for the Alabama Christian Movement for Human Rights.

George Wallace, "Segregation Now, Segregation Forever," January 14, 1963, reprinted with the permission of Allyn and Bacon, Simon and Schuster, Inc.

Martin Luther King, Jr., "Letter From the Birmingham Jail," April 16, 1963, reprinted with the permission of American Friends Service Committee, Philadelphia.

Associated Press photographs, 1963, reprinted with the permission of Associated Press/Wide World Photos.

William, Witherspoon, *Martin Luther King, Jr. . . . To The Mountaintop*, 1985. Reprinted with the permission of Bantam Doubleday Publishing.

Rev. James Bevel, May 2, 1963, reprinted with the permission of Rev. James Bevel.

Photographs and Text, *The Birmingham News*, 1956-1963, reprinted with the permission of *The Birmingham News*, 1998. All rights reserved.

Photographs and Text, *Birmingham Post-Herald*, 1956-1963, reprinted with the permission of the *Birmingham Post-Herald*.

Photographs and Records, Birmingham Public Library, Department of Archives and Manuscripts, reprinted with the permission of Birmingham Public Library.

Photographs, *Birmingham World*, 1963-1964, reprinted with the permission of the *Birmingham World*.

Photographs by Charles Moore, 1963, reprinted with the permission of Black Star.

Photographs and text from "They Challenge Segregation At Its Core," Anne Braden, 1959, reprinted with the permission of Anne Braden.

Howard K. Smith, "Who Speaks for Birmingham," March 16, 1961. Copyright © CBS News, Inc.

Robert Gutwillig, "Six Days In Alabama" *Mademoiselle*, September, 1963, reprinted courtesy Mademoiselle. Copyright © 1963 by The Conde Nast Publications, Inc.

Photographs, United Press International, 1963, reprinted with the permission of United Press International and Corbis-Bettmann Archives.

Photographs, Reuben Davis Collection, 1956 and 1958, reprinted with the permission of Reuben Davis.

Glenn Eskew, *The Alabama Christian Movement for Human Rights and the Birmingham Struggle for Civil Rights*, 1989. Reprinted with the permission of Dr. Glenn Eskew.

Trezzvant W. Anderson, "Dixie's Most Fearless Freedom Fighter Shuttlesworth is Leaving Ala!," reprinted with the permission of G. R. M. Associates, Inc., agents for *The Pittsburgh Courier*. Copyright © 1964 by *The Pittsburgh Courier*: copyright renewed 1992 by *The New Pittsburgh Courier*.

John F. Kennedy, "Address to the Nation," June 11, 1963, reprinted with the permission of the John F. Kennedy Library, Boston.

Martin Luther King, Jr., "I Have A Dream," August 28, 1963, reprinted with the permission of Intellectual Properties Management, Atlanta, Georgia, as manager for the King estate.

Photographs by Danny Lyons, 1963, reprinted with the permission of Magnum Photos, Inc.

Photograph, *The Montgomery Advertiser*, 1956, reprinted with the permission of *The Montgomery Advertiser*.

"Boycott in Birmingham, Ala. . . .," *Newsweek*, May 14, 1962. Copyright © Newsweek, Inc. All rights reserved. Reprinted by permission.

"Fear and Hatred Grip Birmingham," *The New York Times*, April 12, 1960. Copyright © 1960 by The New York Times Company. Reprinted by permission.

Photographs by Lynn Pelham, *Saturday Evening Post*, 1962, reprinted with the permission of Lynn Pelham.

"Birmingham: Integration's Hottest Crucible," *Time* Magazine, Copyright © 1958, Time Inc. Reprinted by permission.

Photograph, *Life* Magazine, January 17, 1958, May and September 1963, reprinted with the permission of Time, Inc..

Andrew M. Manis quote, *A Fire You Can't Put Out: The Civil Rights Life of Birmingham's Fred Shuttlesworth*, 1999. Reprinted with the permission of University of Alabama Press.

Andrew Young quote, *And Birmingham*, 1971, reprinted with the permission of Andrew Young.

Photograph, WABT-TV Newsreel Picture, September 9, 1957, reprinted with the permission of WVTM-TV.

*For assistance with photographs for publication and permissions* for use of copyrighted material: Victoria Bane, *Montgomery Advertiser*; Don Bowden, *Associated Press/Wide World Photo*; Victor Hansen III, Bobby Brandenburg, Von Cille Williams, *The Birmingham News*; Carrie Chalmers, *Magnum Photos, Inc.*; *Newsweek; Conde Nast Publications*; Katherine Driscoll, *United Press International*; Laura Giammarco, *Time/Life Syndicated*; Sharon Minix, *U. M. I. Microfilm*; Mary Morel, *Time/Life Syndicated*; Gloria Mosesson, *The Courier*; Lynn Pelham, *Pelham Photograph Services, Inc.*; Richard Serviss, *Black Star*; Michael Stier, *Corbis/Bettmann Archives*; Neil Waldman, *CBS News Archives*. Copyrighted materials may be reproduced only with the written permission of the agencies listed.

# Index